WHY CAREER ADVICE SUCKS

Cover Design: Tugboat Design

Cover Photo: © VGstockstudio/Shutterstock.com (used with permission)

All charts/graphs used with permission.

Edited by Matthew Wolf

ISBN 978-0-9884053-6-3

EPUB ISBN 978-0-9884053-4-9

Kindle ISBN 978-0-9884053-5-6

Acknowledgments

While there are many who have influenced my thinking on career planning (many of whom I reference in this book), there are several people who particularly challenged me to write and publish this book. And most probably have no knowledge of their impact.

The article in *Fast Company* magazine written by Robert Safian encouraged me that I wasn't alone in my frustration with the ambiguous and unstable career-pathing facing my generation and inspired the subtitle of this book.

Thank you to Listnote (http://khymaera.com) and VoiceBase (http://www.voicebase.com), whose voice-to-text apps helped me compile my notes.

Thank you to Rick Fankhauser at Williams Energy for recognizing and believing in my value as a person and leader long before almost anyone else did.

Thank you to Deborah at Tugboat Design for the cover art on this book. If you need any book cover design, please contact Deborah at tugboatdesign.net.

Thank you to my lovely wife Carolyn, who helped me refine this book. To my three children, Josiah, Reagan, and Dominic, thank you for affording me the liberty to be a child at heart.

Thank you to Matthew Wolf, my brilliant editor! You were an extraordinary help in so many ways. I could not have polished this book without your invaluable effort.

Thank you to everyone else with whom I have had the privilege to cross paths; you have all impacted my life in some way that has contributed to this work.

And last but not least, thank you to Christ, without whom I am nothing, even on my best day.

Contents

Despite recession, currency crises, and tremors of financial instability, the pace of disruption is roaring ahead. The frictionless spread of information and the expansion of personal, corporate, and global networks have plenty of room to run. And here's the conundrum: When businesspeople search for the right forecast—the road map and model that will define the next era—no credible long-term picture emerges. There is one certainty, however. The next decade or two will be defined more by fluidity than by any new, settled paradigm; if there is a pattern to all this, it is that there is no pattern. The most valuable insight is that we are, in a critical sense, in a time of chaos.

To thrive in this climate requires a whole new approach because some people will thrive. They are the members of Generation Flux. This is less a demographic designation than a psychographic one: What defines GenFlux is a mind-set that embraces instability, that tolerates—and even enjoys— recalibrating careers, business models, and assumptions. Not everyone will join Generation Flux, but to be successful, businesses and individuals will have to work at it. This is no simple task. The vast bulk of our institutions—educational, corporate, political—are not built for flux. Few traditional career tactics train us for an era where the most important skill is the ability to acquire new skills.

ROBERT SAFIAN

Introduction

More than ever before, successful career planning means riding the wave of change. Robert Safian coined the term Generation Flux in a February 2012 article in *Fast Company* magazine to describe those who relish riding the wave. It is important to note that the term is psychographic, not demographic: Generation Flux is not defined by age group but by their ability to adapt and remain flexible in the face of a tremendous onslaught of chaotic change.

And it is this current state of flux in which we find our careers sloshing around which has caused quite a bit of uncertainty and has made me ask the question that was the inspiration for the title of this book, *Why Career Advice Sucks*. While many of the old career planning rules no longer apply, far too many career advice experts, counselors, coaches, and even parents either extol the old ways partially or even fully, mostly because it's familiar and what worked for them. But this advice is failing us, leaving many of us befuddled by the new paradigm.

So what are we to do?

First, we must accept the tectonic shift that has already and is still continuing to occur. We cannot afford to stick our proverbial ostrich head in the sand, else a successful career may sail right by us. Second, we have to change how we seek employment and more actively manage our career.

But make no mistake about it; the change foisted upon us is stressful. This is true all the way down to the level of biology. If you give an organism a consistent environment, unchanging levels of temperature, moisture, nutrients, and threats, it will adjust itself to succeed in that environment. If the environment begins to change frequently or rapidly or both, the organism doesn't know what to expect and goes into a state of high alert. Stress is the name we give to this high-alert state. In the short term, it keeps the organism alive, but in the long term, it's a killer. No wonder many people view change and stress as the enemy. But as important as it is to escape or relieve stress, it's important to remember that the stress reaction serves a vital purpose. You can't survive in the long term if you die in the short term.

The surest way to ensure extinction is to resist change and adaptation.

The key to career success now and in the future is to adapt to the ever-changing environment. And continue to change it will. We should neither pretend that change isn't happening nor allow the need for constant adaptation to overwhelm us. Generation Flux is agile and resilient, quick to pivot away from unsuccessful strategies and tough enough to handle setbacks. They are not afraid to fail, since failures are inevitable, and adaptation requires failure. They realize that career success will look different and will be won differently than in the past.

The career lifecycle is spinning faster and faster as the economy changes ever more rapidly, and this lifecycle follows this repeating progression.

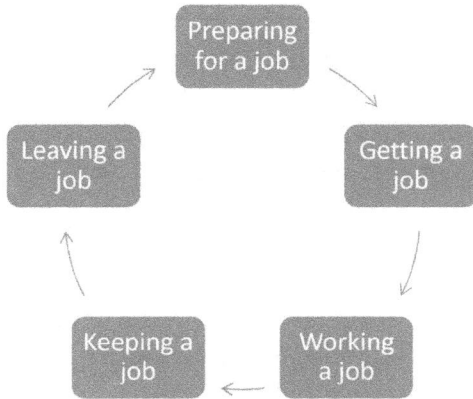

Figure 1

Every job is temporary.

CAREEREALISM.COM

A generation ago, someone might have passed through the cycle only once. Having to prepare for a new job was considered a failure, even a disaster. We need to abandon that stigma on both the employee and employer side of things. The environment has changed, and success requires rapid adaptation. This is the new normal. Of course, the boundaries between these stages are blurred. For example, your experiences while working a job should be preparing you for your next job. So don't be surprised if the discussion of one stage starts bleeding into another.

Adaptability is the name of the game; if you understand that you must now be adaptable and flexible, you will find a way to succeed in your career. If not, you will succumb to job market pressures. We can no longer rely on a decent blue-collar job in manufacturing or a white collar job in another industry where if we just go to work and do a good job we will make a decent living wage and be able to support a family. This simply is not the case anymore, and the sooner we wake up and start enhancing our skills in niche areas (where others aren't focusing), the more successful we will all be. Yes, it has gotten harder to manage a career from job to job to job to job, but it also affords us a lot more opportunity than in previous generations to work in many more different and varied industries and companies.

While there are definitely drawbacks to today's job environment, there is genuine, incredible opportunity out there. At times, managing our career path might seem daunting. I fully relate because I've been frustrated in my own career. Take a minute to look at my LinkedIn profile: www.linkedin.com/in/milesanthony-smith. I recognize that my career path is by no means the only way to do it, but you can see how I have used flexibility and adaptability to find opportunities that would utilize my skills and talents in spite of the fact that I've had many very different job titles and industries. It's up to us to determine what path we are going to take and chart that course. Make no mistake, it will be an interesting course, not necessarily easy, with its share of ups and downs, but it has the potential to be a more varied, worthwhile, and meaningful career than previous generations experienced.

To thank you for purchasing the paperback or ebook version of *Why Career Advice Sucks*, I am giving you my audiobook on a completely complimentary basis! Whoa, wait a cotton-pickin' minute! "Did I hear you right, Miles?" Yes, you did. All I ask in exchange is that you provide your email address... the one you regularly use (not your generic signup email addy). Hey, I spend a ton of my own time and money recording, editing, mastering, and publishing my audiobook on Audible, iTunes, and Amazon, so it's only fair for you to supply me with a real email address, and I'm happy to provide you with the complimentary audiobook in exchange. And it's not an abridged version; it's the entire audiobook.

To get it, go to milesanthonysmith.com/wcas-audiobook and use password GIMMEMYWLS2AUDIOBOOK. Go check it out right now. I'll wait for you to come back to the book! You may want the audiobook version to listen to the contents for the first time or to listen again as a refresher later while you're driving, working out, cooking, washing dishes, buying groceries, shoveling snow, mowing the lawn, eating lunch, doing data entry, waiting at a doctor's office, getting a massage, fishing, painting, or wrapping presents... I think you get the idea that an audiobook can be enjoyed while multitasking; something you can't do with a physical book or ebook!

PART 1

Lies, Damned Lies

Historical Context

The invention of retirement and myth of life-long employment are lies that we have accepted as fact, and until recently, have held mostly true. But now, these mythical constructs are unravelling, challenging millions of workers to change how they think about work and career life. These two lies strike at the very fabric of our desired financial and emotional security. They have been perpetuated over time by some who were well-intentioned and others who were not. But regardless of their origins or motive, we must face the lies and redefine what it means to have a secure and meaningful career.

1

Vanishing Jobs, Middle Class Wages, and Retirement

Labor-saving devices have destroyed many jobs but have given rise to many new ones. It simply is up to us if we are going to resist or embrace the future.

Where have all the jobs gone, especially the ones that pay well and allow us to retire comfortably after twenty or thirty years of continuous employment? It may appear for many job seekers that traditional blue-collar and some white-collar jobs are becoming extinct like the dodo bird. In post-World War II America, with unemployment generally low, blue-collar wage jobs easy to get, and clear routes out of blue-collar jobs into white-collar jobs (i.e., a college degree), it was easy to forget that the job market will continue to change. But as with all nonequilibrium markets, things go along swimmingly until they don't.

Many of the middle-class-paying traditional blue-collar jobs have vanished from the US landscape, having been subject to exportation to countries around the globe, reduction in wages, or elimination due to automation (see Figure 2). The disappearance of these jobs or replacement of them by lower-paying jobs in the US is a source of real pain for individuals and for our overall economy. We should not despair but instead look for opportunities to adapt and evolve. There are many other new job opportunities that exist today and others to come in the future. Highly skilled, technical jobs abound in this new economy. Technical colleges are in many locales working directly with the manufacturing industry to prepare workers, not for routine widget-making, but to monitor and give input to highly complex machines that make the widgets of the future.

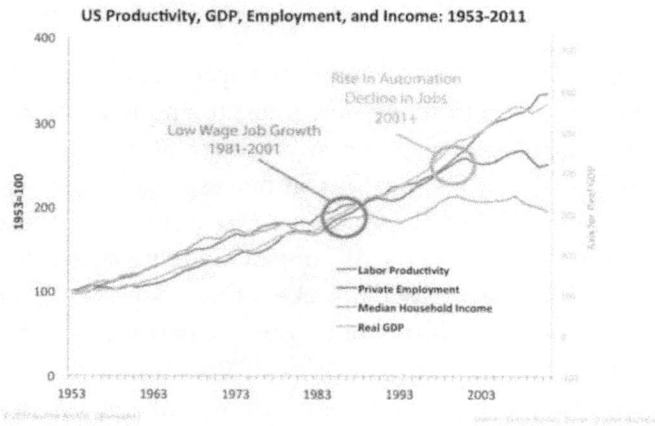

Figure 2

Many people don't want to be a plumber, electrician, carpenter, or other tradesman, but there is currently a shortage of applicants for these types of jobs. And retail positions are plentiful and growing rapidly. It's not that there aren't jobs out there, they just not may be the jobs we want. According to the US Bureau of Labor Statistics (BLS), job growth has increased in retail, technology, service (food, hospitality, janitors), trades (construction, plumbing, electrical), transportation, individual and family services, and healthcare. These and other growing industries are often considered undesirable due to less desirable environmental conditions (manual labor, evening and weekend hours, highly technical). The good paying blue- and white-collar middle-class jobs that we once knew and loved hardly exist anymore. It is true that basic manual labor manufacturing jobs have declined as a percentage of overall jobs, but we still make things in the USA! Highly technical manufacturing workers are in high demand to interact with the technology that has steadily increased manufacturing efficiency over the last seventy years.

It is not only manufacturing that is feeling the pressure of a changing job market. Aside from manufacturing, we have seen employment declines in the following industries: publishers, postal service, travel agencies, bookstores, and federal government. White-collar work was once virtually guaranteed to everyone who managed to get a college degree. The competition for those jobs has increased, of course, as a higher and higher percentage of the population attended college. In the same way that machine technology disrupts existing manufacturing jobs, information technology disrupts jobs that depend on the scarcity of information. When there are a dozen websites begging you to book your own flight, it suddenly seems crazy to pay a travel agent to do it for you.

> There will be many things that machines can't do, such as services that require thinking, creativity, synthesizing, problem-solving, and innovating. . . . Advances in AI and robotics allow people to cognitively offload repetitive tasks and invest their attention and energy in

things where humans can make a difference.
We already have cars that talk to us, a phone
we can talk to, robots that lift the elderly out
of bed, and apps that remind us to call Mom.
An app can dial Mom's number and even send
flowers, but an app can't do that most human
of all things: emotionally connect with her.

PAMELA RUTLEDGE

As in the case of manufacturing, there are still white-collar jobs to be had, but they require more technical skills or skills that are hard to automate. Knowing how to access a particular type of information is less of a distinction: Google is putting it out there for everyone. Higher-level skills such as analyzing and mining the information are what will set you apart. The impact on blue-collar jobs has been well documented over the past decade, but increasing numbers of white-collar jobs are predicted to be negatively impacted by accelerating advances in technology. Concerns from some respondents to the 2014 and 2016 Future of the Internet (compiled by Pew Research and Elon University) are:

1. Displacement of workers from automation is already
   happening—and about to get much worse.

   Everything that can be automated will be
   automated. Non-skilled jobs lacking in
   "human contribution" will be replaced by
   automation when the economics are favorable.
   At the hardware store, the guy who used to
   cut keys has been replaced by a robot. In the

law office, the clerks who used to prepare discovery have been replaced by software. IBM Watson is replacing researchers by reading every report ever written anywhere. This begs the question: What can the human contribute? The short answer is that if the job is one where that question cannot be answered positively, that job is not likely to exist.

ROBERT CANNON

2. The consequences for income inequality will be profound.

The central question of 2025 will be: What are people for in a world that does not need their labor, and where only a minority are needed to guide the 'bot-based economy?

STOWE BOYD

3. We will see a return to uniquely "human" forms of production.

To some degree, this is already happening. In terms of the large-scale, mass-produced economy, the utility of low-skill human workers is rapidly diminishing, as many blue-collar jobs (e.g., in manufacturing) and white-collar jobs (e.g., processing insurance paperwork) can be handled much more cheaply by automated systems. And we can already see some hints of reaction to this trend in the current economy: entrepreneurially-minded unemployed and underemployed people are taking advantages of sites like Etsy and TaskRabbit to market quintessentially human skills. And in response, there is increasing demand for "artisanal" or "hand-crafted" products that were made by a human. In the long run this trend will actually push toward the re-localization and re-humanization of the economy, with the 19th- and 20th-century economies of scale exploited where they make sense (cheap, identical, disposable goods), and human-oriented techniques (both older and newer) increasingly accounting for goods and services that are valuable, customized, or long-lasting.

A NETWORK SCIENTIST FOR BBN TECHNOLOGIES

4. More learning systems will migrate online. Some will be self-directed and some offered or required by employers; others will be hybrid online/real-world classes. Workers will be expected to learn continuously all the while juggling their day-to-day work responsibilities.

5. Tough-to-teach intangible skills, capabilities and attributes such as emotional intelligence, curiosity, creativity, adaptability, resilience and critical thinking will be most highly valued.

6. While the traditional college degree will still hold sway in 2026, more employers may accept alternate credentialing systems, as learning options and their measures evolve while proof of competency will be validated in real-world work portfolios.

7. There will be many millions more people and millions fewer jobs in the future so unemployment numbers will rise.

Admittedly, there are others from this same survey on the other side of the aisle that offer a more rosy view of the future. But I think it is far more important to prepare for the more pessimistic viewpoint and be pleasantly surprised than the other way around. While many jobs are vanishing from the landscape, there are many others being created, which is an incredible opportunity if we choose to seize the day. And with many jobs being eliminated or reduced by the advance of technology and automation, many firms, small or large, will struggle to keep up. Witness the dissolution of more companies than are being started, an alarming trend that started in 2008 according to the US Census Bureau (see Figure 3). For the first time in over thirty years, more companies are closing their doors than new ones opening theirs. Since new firms are the largest driver of new job growth, this is not a good sign for the future of job creation, a major driver of sustainable economic growth.

The U.S. economy has become less entrepreneurial over time
Firm Entry and Exit Rates in the United States, 1978-2011

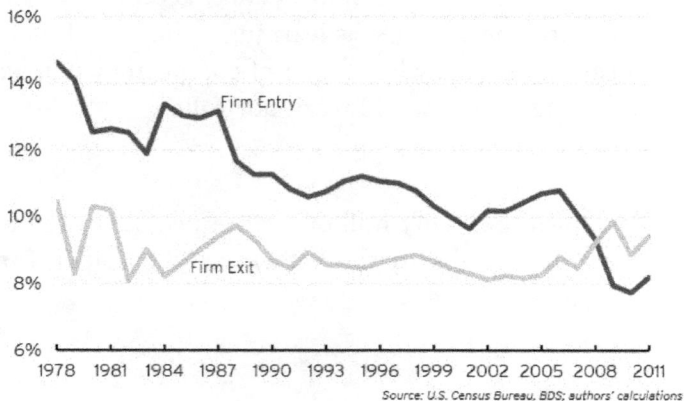

Source: U.S. Census Bureau, BDS; authors' calculations

Figure 3. Source: Brookings Institution

Figure 4 also shows that while job destruction has declined in the wake of the Great Recession, job growth has not grown fast enough to replace all of those lost jobs. And with more unemployed and underemployed workers seeking better employment hours and wages, continued job market challenges abound.

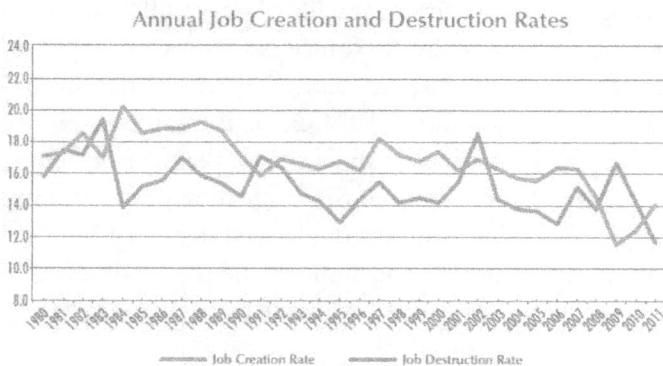

Annual Job Creation and Destruction Rates

Job Creation Rate   Job Destruction Rate

Figure 4. Source: US Census Bureau

The *Two Income Trap* is thick with irony. Middle-class mothers went into the workforce in a calculated effort to give their families an economic edge. Instead, millions of them are now in the workplace just so their families can break even. If two-income families had saved the second paycheck, they would have built a different kind of safety net—the kind that comes from having plenty of money in the bank. But families didn't save that money. Even as millions of mothers marched into the workforce, savings declined, and not because families were frittering away their paychecks on toys for themselves or their children. Instead, families were swept up in a bidding war, competing furiously with one another for their most important possession: a house in a decent school district. But the frenzied bidding wars, fueled by families with two incomes, changed the game for single-income families as well, pushing them down the economic ladder.

Our research eventually unearthed one stunning fact. The families in the worst financial trouble are not the usual suspects. They are not the very young, tempted by the freedom of their first credit cards. They are not the elderly, trapped by failing bodies and declining savings accounts. And they are not a random assortment of Americans who lack the self-control to keep their spending in check.

The average two-income family earns far more today than did the single-breadwinner family of a generation ago. And yet, once they

> have paid the mortgage, the car payments, the
> taxes, the health insurance, and the day-care
> bills, today's dual-income families have less
> discretionary income—and less money to put
> away for a rainy day—than the single-income
> family of a generation ago.

SENATOR ELIZABETH WARREN

As real wages have stagnated over the last twenty years, and food, housing, and clothing inflation has grown, the cost of necessities as a percentage of household income has caused families' budgets to tighten. While merely a couple of decades ago a middle-class family could subsist on one income, it now takes two incomes, according to Senator Elizabeth Warren's book *The Two Income Trap*. In order to have the same standard of living of a generation ago, families are forced to have two incomes, and as Senator Warren shows from her research, this is not as a result of too many families overspending. The pressure that this places on pursuing our careers ends up being challenging, frustrating, and even hazardous to our health.

Many pundits rail against the fact that not enough people are saving money for future rainy days with the idea of retirement seemingly more unattainable for workers today. It is often assumed that people are lazy and choosing not to save like they used to ten, twenty, thirty, forty years ago. Real wages (adjusted for inflation) have remained pretty flat, so there is some truth to the fact, but it is been complicated by other factors (such as the employment outlook) over the last twenty years that have made it much harder just to get by. So be careful about judging the Generations X and Y for not saving for retirement, or judging the Boomer generation for complaining about the challenges they face. Things are getting harder for the Boomer generation, but it is that much harder for the younger generations.

> The notion of retiring at 65 when the life expectancy reaches 100 is neither a realistic economic model nor a socially-engaged community model.
>
> HEATHER MCGOWAN

The construct of retirement is dubious at best and a farce at worst. Expectations contrary to this are to be dashed.

Whether you are a fan of "defined benefit" (pension) retirement plans or "defined contribution" (401k, IRA, etc.) plans, almost no one would argue against older generations retiring at some point to reap the benefits of an earned break from employment. But why does our culture focus so intently on this idea of retirement, which wasn't even considered until the late nineteenth and early twentieth centuries? When the construct of retirement was first introduced in 1889 in Germany, the life expectancy was 45 years old; now it is 77 in Germany. And in 1935, when the US set up its social security system, the retirement age was 65 with life expectancy being 68. It was a benefit for a choice few retirees who lived longer than the average. With today's average life expectancy in the US at nearly 80, it is easy to see why retirement and healthcare costs are ballooning. No one wants to deal with the uncomfortable fact that most people would never retire under the US system created in 1935. As life expectancy has dramatically increased, governments have sought to extend the age at which workers can qualify for public retirement benefits, but that has not been enough to deal with the exploding financial liability of government to retirees.

On top of this, there is convincing research that points to a correlation between retiring completely (i.e., not continuing even part-time work) and earlier onset of greater health conditions (and thus greater costs).[1] Even members of the military and police force are able to retire after twenty years of service, with many of them having two incomes in their mid-forties or early fifties (one pension and one new full-time job). I am not begrudging our military and police force, who routinely put their lives in harm's way, their pension; they have earned it. I am merely shining light on an area that needs reform in order to stave off a crisis between the pensioners (private or public) and those working to support them (younger generations). We don't need social class warfare to get worse than it already is. De-escalation is needed by reforming the system to treat workers of different ages justly.

2

Generational Transition

Will each future generation continue to enjoy
a better quality of life than its immediate
predecessor? In developing countries that have
not yet reached the technological frontier, the
answer is almost certainly yes. In advanced
economies, though the answer should still be
yes, the challenges are becoming formidable.

KENNETH ROGOFF

Many of Generations X and Y (aka Millennials), who
grew up during the go-go years of the nineties and early
aughts, look at what has happened to the job market
with horror. We long for those "good ol' days" when
it seemed easier to get a job, stay in a job (life-long
employment), find a better job, or find a better paying
job. With those days firmly behind us, it is easy to be
resentful of the Boomer and Great Generations because
they've had an easier time finding and retaining good
employment—receiving peak levels of income and benefits that came with that employment (pensions, zero-
cost health insurance, stock options that only went up,
etc.). And according to a book by Landon Jones,
Boomers are the wealthiest, most active, and most
physically fit generation compared to previous generations.[2] The reason to draw these distinctions between
Boomers and Generations X, Y, or Z is not to increase

class warfare but merely to put into context the past, present, and future challenges facing the various generations.

While nearly every generation thinks they have it harder than the previous one, there is a genuine sense that the younger generations of X and Y will not be as upwardly mobile economically as their parents and grandparents. Some will climb to a higher level, but many will fight to stay stable or slide downward. This certainly has happened to some extent with other generations, but the stable and downward trends will grow at a faster and alarming rate. That's something that is different from the Boomer generation in general. While Generations X and Y are having to work harder AND smarter than previous generations did early in their career, Boomers have recently run into their own career challenges, such as delayed retirement, age discrimination, etc. The accelerating pace of change will not be kind to older or younger generations. And no matter what generation we belong to, we all have a choice to recognize the situation we find ourselves in and do our best to make it better. This might involve working a second job or starting a side business while working a full-time job. There are opportunities out there. If you seek them, don't give up, and choose to persevere, you will find them.

I want to share some statistics about Millennials, not because this book is directed only at them, but because their experience most clearly illustrates the dramatic changes we are living through. Millennials' living habits are evolving as a result of the current job market, which has had a profound economic and psychological effect on both them and their Boomer parents. According to a 2016 study by the Pew Research Center (see Figure

5), more Millennials are living with their parents than any other generation, some of them either unemployed, underemployed, or sadly unemployable due to a lack of work ethic.

Millennials are the generation most likely to live at home

% of 25- to 35-year-olds living in parent(s) home

Millennials in 2016	15%
Gen Xers in 2000	10
Late Boomers in 1990	11
Early Boomers in 1981	8
Silents in 1964	8

Note: "Living in parent(s) home" means residing in a household headed by a parent.
Source: Pew Research Center analysis of 1964, 1981, 1990, 2000 and 2016 Current Population Survey, Annual Social and Economic Supplements.

PEW RESEARCH CENTER

Figure 5. Pew Research Center, © 2016,
http://www.pewsocialtrends.org/2016/05/24/for-first-time-in-modern-era-living-with-parents-edges-out-other-living-arrangements-for-18-to-34-year-olds/

The challenge is that while some children need to move back home after the first time they leave, too many parents allow them to overstay their welcome rather than challenge them to leave the nest again after they recover from whatever brought them back home (divorce, financial challenge, unemployment, etc.). If children stay in the protective bubble of Mom and Dad's house too long, they risk becoming underemployable or unemployable due to being spoiled and lacking a strong work ethic. If returning home is needed, I do not reject this outright, but as job seekers who should have a sense of pride and accomplishment in living independently, we need to be careful not to abuse our parent's generosity and overstay our welcome. Let's endeavor to make these truly short return stays, even if our parents want us to stay longer.

As a result of financial struggles and changing opinions about marriage, more Millennials are delaying marriage to a later age or choosing to remain single. This depresses their own economic condition, as well as that of the country as a whole, since there are fewer consumer purchases associated with marriage and children (homes, vehicles, appliances, clothing, etc.). There are numerous studies showing that marriage results in higher accumulation of wealth, not just economic consumption; one such study was performed by Jay Zagorsky at Ohio State University. His study shows that married couples have up to four times the wealth of their single or divorced counterparts (double the wealth for each spouse, which is quadruple when you combine the two). There are many reasons for this, among them that couples are able to pool their financial resources, reduce double expenses (home, appliances, health insurance, etc.), allow one spouse to work more hours than the other (something single parents are unable to do). The catch is that this wealth advantage is for those whose marriages have worked out, not for those who have been divorced; divorcees' wealth is worse than those who remained single. While the divorce rate has remained stable in recent years, the marriage rate has declined steeply. This may be one reason why more Millennials are delaying or abstaining from marriage. If marriage is a gamble (you could end up better off than you are now, but you could end up worse off), and the odds of successful marriage are getting worse, it seems to make more sense to keep your options open.

Yet there are ways to increase the benefits of marriage and decrease the risk of it failing. To start, it will help if one can make the marriage decision based a bit more on reason and logic (e.g., does this potential partner have the same values, ideas about child rearing, spending money, etc.) and less on emotion. If you rule out marriage until you're, say, 27 and feel mature enough for it, you miss out on the chance to have marriage itself mature you in ways that don't happen otherwise. I am not saying everyone should get married young, but I married at 20 and started having children at 24. As a result, I am less self-centered, more motivated to work hard (financial motivation), and more engaged in serving others' needs above my own. I repeat—I am not arguing that everyone must marry young or at all, but a well-chosen marriage actually gives you far more flexibility and resilience in the face of never-ending waves of change. Even if one spouse loses their job, the other might be able to provide support until employment can be secured. We simply don't know if, when, or how long unemployment or underemployment will visit its wrath upon us, but from personal experience, I can tell you that it WILL come at some point in your or your spouse's career. While this thought is not comforting to those who are just getting started in your career or have not experienced this, it is a reality that we must choose to face, so we aren't in shock when it happens. Shock usually causes us to go into a paralyzed state of inaction where we seem to be in quicksand. This is a perilous position and one that might be more easily avoided by having a spouse to listen and coach you through the emotional challenge.

3

Income Inequality?

An imbalance between rich and poor is the oldest and most fatal ailment of all republics.

PLUTARCH, GREEK HISTORIAN, FIRST CENTURY AD

Income inequality is a major topic of discussion in the US today. And it's not a pleasant one, with accusations of greed, jealousy, and envy flying from both sides. The real danger with income inequality is that at some point if wages are too low, relative to the standard cost of living (food, fuel, housing, etc.) being too high, social unrest will break out. Research by the New England Complex Systems Institute indicates that when food inflation approaches a high enough level, people turn to violent protests, riots, and general unrest. This research actually predicted the Arab Spring weeks before it happened. This has had implications for countries around the world, but it could cause unrest right here in the US if things get much worse. Wage and good prices are relative to one another and are truly in the eye of the beholder, and while things are challenging in the US job market, we certainly have it far better than many developed and emerging markets.

Studies from Columbia University and the
Congressional Budget Office and others in the
last two years indicate that income inequality
has actually lessened . . . not increased . . .
because of the impact of government transfer
payments. What irritates people is that the 1%
have been able to stretch their lead even more,
especially through the recent downturn.
When they speak of a "decades-long slide in
equality," people are referring to pure "money
income," which doesn't include the impact of
relative taxes and government transfer
payments. When those are considered,
inequality has declined. The key to increasing
the welfare of the poor, studies show, is
policies and an environment that foster job
creation.

PHIL HAUCK

According to the US Census Bureau, real (adjusting for
inflation) median household income is basically where
it was in 1988 (see Figure 6). This means that we have
a generation of people scraping by on their household
income that, following the temporary growth period
from 1996 to 2007, has returned to 1988 levels. There
are endless anecdotal examples of families struggling to
make ends meet, taking part-time instead of full-time
jobs, living with relatives, and surviving on unemployment and/or food stamps (Supplemental Nutritional
Assistance Program or SNAP). While previous generations could assume a continually growing standard of

living, many are now facing the reality that their real household incomes have stagnated, or, worse yet, fallen.

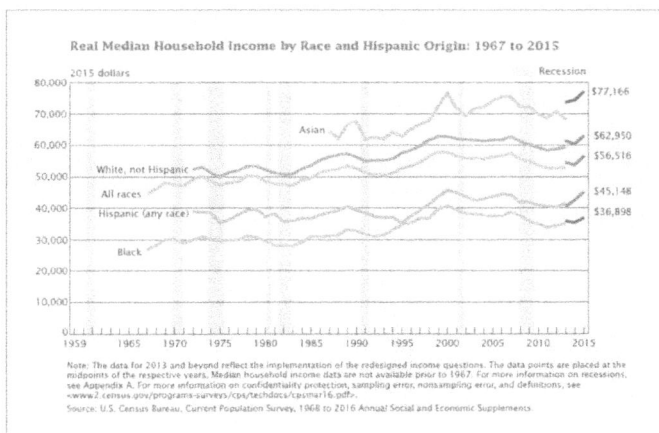

Figure 6

There is more to this story, however. Real median household incomes (see Figure 6) do not include government transfer payments (Medicare, Medicaid, welfare, food stamps, unemployment, student grants, retirement, disability payments, veterans' payments, and education/training) nor do they include subsidies (such as those received by farmers, exporters, and manufacturers). These payments have a very real impact on how much income people have to spend. Transfer payments and subsidies are a form of wealth redistribution, especially considering how broadly they apply to many people groups in society. Transfer payments have grown steadily since 1970 and exponentially since 2000 on a gross basis. And our disposable incomes are made up of a larger and larger percentage of transfer payments (see Figure 6). Not good news for the long term growth of our economy.

23

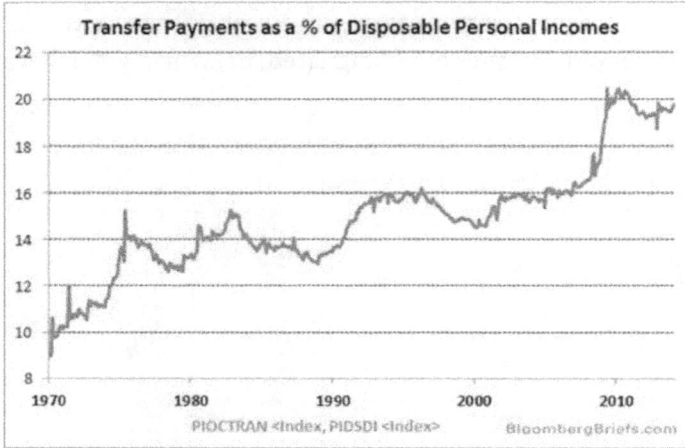

Figure 6: Used with permission of Bloomberg L.P. Copyright © 2014. All rights reserved.

In ten states and the District of Columbia, welfare pays more than the entry-level salary for a teacher in that state. In 38 states and the District of Columbia, welfare is more generous than the average starting salary for a secretary. And in the three most generous states, welfare pays more than the wages for an entry-level computer programmer. In eight states, welfare recipients receive benefits worth more than the median salary there. This is not even to consider the other costs of going to work.

MICHAEL D. TANNER

There is a growing disincentive for the middle and lower classes to work. According to a 2013 study by the CATO Institute, those on welfare benefits would in most cases need to earn considerably more than minimum wage in order to net the same wages (after taxes) as opposed to continuing to receive welfare, which includes TANF, food stamps (SNAP), Medicaid, housing assistance, WIC, energy assistance (LIHEAP), and free commodities. When controlling for taxes (of which there are none for welfare), in Hawaii workers would need to make over $60,590 annually just to break even with welfare benefits. And while Hawaii is the most generous welfare state, it is not hard to see that we have a disincentive to work. This does not imply that those that are on welfare are lazy or second-class citizens; many people have needed help during a tough time in their life. But we want to provide incentives for welfare recipients to find work that will pay them more than the state is providing.

When taking into account transfer payments, real household incomes have not been impacted nearly as much as the first chart in this chapter (Figure 6) would seem to indicate. However, inflation of prices of goods and services have far outstripped the increase in wages of those who don't receive transfer payments. And it is those middle-class people that are working as hard as they can but can't seem to get ahead that we should be most concerned about. According to the USDA, participation in the US for food stamps (SNAP) has grown from over 26 million people in 2007 to 47 million people in 2013, at a cost of $33 billion and nearly $80 billion, respectively. This is an alarming growth rate by an order of magnitude that far exceeds any previous economic downturns going back to 1969 when the SNAP program was started. And according to a 2013 report by Pew Charitable Trusts, Generation X lost 45% of their

net worth from 2007 to 2010, which will create head-
winds for their ability to attain or sustain middle-class
status, let alone have enough money for a decent retirement. On top of this, families will have less money to
send their children to college, which will affect future
generations of workers as well, further compounding
our current career challenge.

America's Shrinking Middle Class

Percent of adults self-identifing as each social class

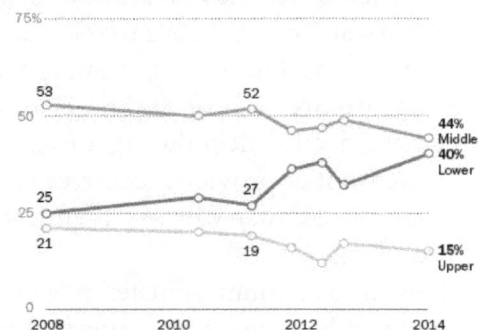

75%

53 / 52 / 44% Middle / 40% Lower

25 / 27

21 / 19 / 15% Upper

2008   2010   2012   2014

Note: "Lower" includes lower-middle class and lower class; "upper" includes
upper-middle class and upper class.
PEW RESEARCH CENTER

Figure 8. Pew Research Center, "Despite recovery, fewer Americans
identify as middle class," © 2014, http://www.pewresearch.org/fact-
tank/2014/01/27/despite-recovery-fewer-americans-identify-as-
middle-class/

The flip side of our lower wages is that as we have
outsourced jobs to China, India, and other nations, we
have seen the cost of goods from those regions decline
in nominal or real (inflation-adjusted) terms. This is a
very real benefit that many Americans forget when they
reflect on their paycheck. While discarding free trade
agreements and enacting tariffs and taxes on imports
sounds good to both pro-labor groups and to the aver-

26

age American, previous protectionist actions in US and world history have almost always not benefited the average blue- or white-collar worker. Protectionist rhetoric might win at the ballot box, but when viewed as a cost per job saved, it isn't worth it. Consider this: in 2011 the US placed a high tariff on foreign tires to save tire-manufacturing jobs in electorally important places like Ohio. The tariffs saved 1,200 jobs at the most—at a cost of $900,000 per job saved. This is a terribly inefficient way to protect the American worker from foreign competition.

> The goal should not be equality of income or wealth but equality of opportunity. The role of government should be to make sure the playing field is level and the rules are simple and fair.
>
> JOHN MAULDIN

As we have seen, it's hard to get a clear picture of what the true state of income inequality is in the US. Ultimately, we need to be more concerned about making sure the government allows equal economic opportunity than trying to engineer equal economic results. Some areas for significant improvement at the federal level are equality of education via reform (currently being fiercely resisted by teachers' unions) and equality of our economic and legal system (removing government favoritism and crony capitalism). At the local level, while the squeezing of the middle class makes things more challenging than in previous generations, we should be motivated to find the career opportunities amidst the difficult environment. We cannot simply rely on politicians to redistribute wealth through various government programs. Tempting as that latter option is, making the middle class dependent on government largesse will only further push America into debt. It will not bring the economic revival we need that comes from American ingenuity and entrepreneurship.

4

Uncertainty: Government Regulation and Labor Markets

What scares so many organizations (for-profit and non-profit alike) these days is that the direction of government policy is either uncertain or known to be anti-growth. Government regulation is already high in almost every industry, and the prevailing wisdom is that this already burdensome regulatory environment will only get worse as legislators are more and more out of touch with the average organization. With this much economic policy uncertainty (see Figure 9), it's no wonder organizations aren't creating the new jobs needed to nurse a wounded economy back to life.

As our "muddle through" economy plods forward with much uncertainty surrounding government policy, global concern is being raised about out of control government deficit spending and manipulation of markets via quantitative easing (aka printing money). With dramatically exploding government debt (expected to be $30 trillion by the end of 2027 in the US alone), looming future unfunded liabilities ($200-250 trillion for social security and Medicare, etc.), and a Federal Reserve balance sheet that has grown over 444% since 2007 (from a paltry $900,000 to $4 trillion), politicians will be faced with reducing government transfer payments or increasing taxes, both of which are political hot potatoes. But the easier of the two routes is to tax the rich, since reducing benefits to the poor is harder to sell on the news. As a result, many tax deductions will be significantly reduced or eliminated in the future as a result of our government continuing to live beyond its means.

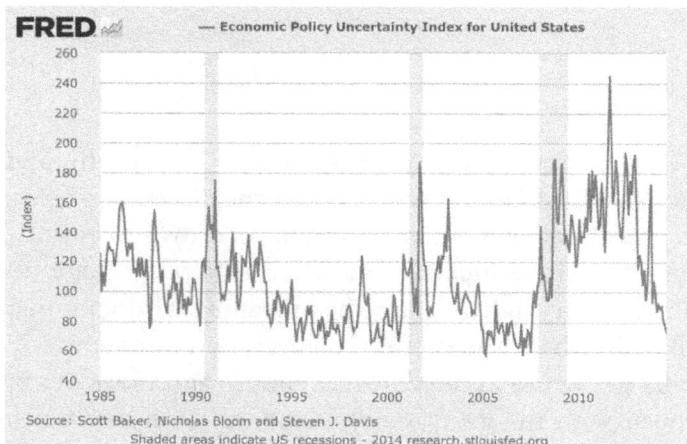

Figure 9

Added to increasing government policy and spending/ taxation uncertainty, havoc has been created in labor force participation and competition, leading to a reallocation of labor, both domestically in the US and abroad amongst other countries, that has and will continue to alter the nature and pay of jobs as far into the future as we can see.

The labor force participation rate peaked at 67.1% in 2000, declined to 64.1% in 2010, and is projected to decline further to somewhere between 58.5% and 61.5% in 2040 as the result of a tougher job market (see Figure 10). This implies that many more will be pushed out of the active workforce onto already stressed governmental or family assistance. What is surprising is that labor force participation for women increased steadily over the last forty years, while the participation rate for men has declined steadily over the same timeframe. And while it would be too simplistic to say that women are simply taking jobs away from men, it is an alarming trend.

Labor Force Participation Rates: 1948-2050

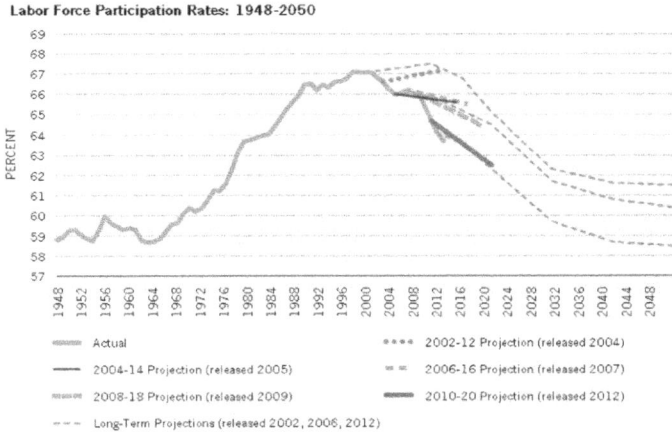

Figure 10. Source: Federal Reserve Bank of St. Louis

One of the things that is challenging in the job market is that active labor participation rates fluctuate based on how competitive wages are relative to another country, industry, or company. If wages in a particular place are uncompetitive (i.e., they are high compared to another place), labor reallocates itself. Under normal circumstances, this is a regular occurrence. As technology or information changes, businesses or industries have to adjust to remain competitive. The challenge we find ourselves in today is that the pace of change has been accelerating and shows no signs of slowing down. When one country's wages become too uncompetitive, job markets in that country can slow down or grind to a halt in extreme cases. This helps us understand why countries in Europe have gone through the financial hardship that they did. Essentially their labor markets were priced too high (inflated by unsustainable private and public debt levels), so people were making more in wages than the market would've reflected naturally.

You can keep this game of musical chairs going for a while by government absorbing more debt to "prop up" the economy, thereby artificially inflating wages during the boom cycle. At some point, however, the game of "kick the can down the road" is over, and wages must come back into equilibrium. This results in a bust cycle as wages come back into line with reality. Certain European countries' labor markets have recently been overvalued relative to others, and those countries are having to come back in the line with their neighboring European countries. And to some extent that's what's happening in the US, with certain industries and job types becoming uncompetitive, resulting in reduced wages. This has certainly happened in manufacturing industries as well as others. That is another political hot potato, since people don't want to face reality and learn how to fix the problem. And this hasn't been all bad news. As manual jobs are becoming more and more automated by machinery and technology, we have more highly skilled (and higher paying) manufacturing jobs than we have ever had before for those willing to apply themselves to learning more complex work. Things always change, and whether or not we adapt to those will determine whether or not we will be successful in the future.

While it may take fifty to one hundred years or more, eventually global wage parity will take place, which will have as much of a profound economic impact on our society as the global economic upheaval we currently find ourselves in. This won't necessarily happen in every country in the world, but when it happens in a "critical mass" of the world (as more emerging markets switch to developed, mature markets), the arbitrage of importing cheaper goods via cheaper labor from other countries will cease as the wages of the currently emerging economies rise (as they almost always do) to a point near equilibrium (wage parity) with developed countries' wages as they decline.

The labor market has been in turmoil the last few years, contributing to a stubbornly high unemployment rate that has climbed to record levels (with a small decline recently). With nearly 7 million people unemployed and 22 million additional underemployed (part-time instead of full-time), we are facing a crisis not seen in several generations. This further depresses wages for non-skilled workers, creating an employer's market for low-skill jobs and causing the middle and lower classes to suffer lower wages than a generation ago. The only remedy is to learn and adapt skills that cannot be outsourced or automated. As you can see from Figure 11, the yardstick by which we measure unemployment in the US has changed over the years. The U3 is what the BLS currently uses, but it does not include short-term discouraged workers, marginally attached workers, and part-time workers who would prefer full-time work. The Shadow Stats version is the broadest measure, including long-term discouraged workers, and is the most reflective of unemployment and all underemployment combined. The Great Recession has created underemployment that is not reported in the news. We are creating a permanent underclass of people who are

on public assistance indefinitely. And while we need
some kind of a stop-gap safety net for those who have
fallen on hard times financially, our economy can't fully
rebound without a significant decrease in unemployment AND underemployment.

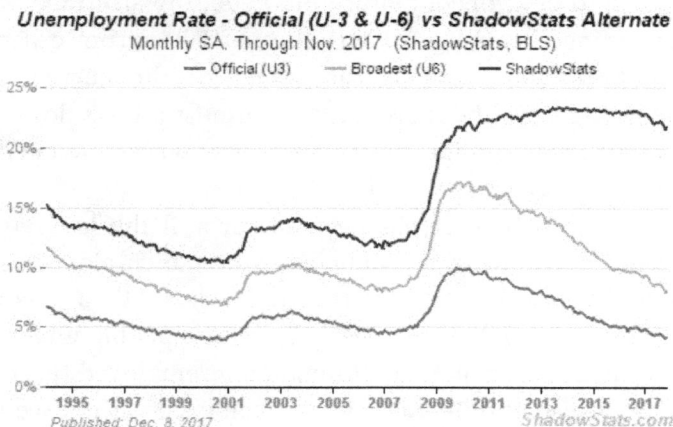

Figure 11. Courtesy of ShadowStats.com

Long-term unemployment is a terrifying trap.
Once you've been out of work for six months,
there's little you can do to find work.
Employers put you at the back of the jobs line,
regardless of how strong the rest of your
resume is. After all, they usually don't even
look at it.

MATTHEW O'BRIEN

Recent research by Rand Ghayad and William Dickens
of Northeastern University indicates that the labor mar-

ket is broken. It used to be that there wasn't any marked difference in the ability to get a call for an interview for those who have been unemployed six months or more and those unemployed six months or less. Now, however, the most important factor determining whether you will get an interview is how long you have been unemployed. Other potential discrimination factors such as your race, age, gender, education, etc., are not nearly as important as length of unemployment. And factors like how much job hopping a candidate has done or whether they have industry experience are trumped by being unemployed six months or more.

What we risk as a society is having the long-term unemployed become completely unemployable. That would be a double whammy on the economy, a drag on social programs (government transfer payments) compounded by the lack of economic productivity (lowering national GDP and diminishing earned wages). Ghayad's and Dickens's research seems to indicate that we have structural unemployment that won't be significantly impacted by job training or a stronger economy in the short term. This doesn't mean that all hope is lost if you have been out of work longer than six months; it just means that you have more to overcome. For those of us who *are* gainfully employed, it should make us even more thankful to have a job.

Be careful about judging someone who is out of work. You might think that the reason they can't find employment is that they're not employable, or they're bad at their job, or they're not open to available job opportunities. From the outside, we really don't know the specifics, and it's just too easy to oversimplify the situation and pass judgment on them. I have been on both sides of the aisle; I know that it's hard to find a new position right at the moment you need it. I've been on the other side, judging other people and discounting their job skills. It's way too easy to judge when we ought to remain compassionate and understanding.

My career has seen its share of challenges, including three bouts of unemployment (lasting from three to nine months). Each time I eventually landed a new position, but each situation had its unique challenges and required its unique solution. From personal experience, I can tell you that subsequent bouts of unemployment do not get easier; if anything, each one gets harder emotionally. But all is not lost; we just have to keep our head down and persevere. Each time, it was scary, stressful, and nerve-wracking, but I survived, never got behind on my bills (thanks to God), and increased my resilience in the process. It strained, then strengthened my marriage and other relationships. In one case, I had to pay the hefty penalty to draw on my 401k retirement account (which I don't recommend unless you are in dire circumstances). While I don't ever want to go through another round of unemployment, I sincerely wouldn't trade those experiences for all the money in the world.

5

Wrap-up: Craving Simplicity and Certainty

The greatest danger is one that may not be faced for decades but that is lurking out there. The United States was built on the assumption that a rising tide lifts all ships. That has not been the case for the past generation, and there is no indication that this socio-economic reality will right itself any time soon. That means that a core assumption is at risk. The problem is that social stability has been built around this assumption—not on the assumption that everyone is owed a living, but the assumption that on the whole, all benefit from growing productivity and efficiency.

At the same time, the United States faces a potentially significant but longer-term geopolitical problem deriving from economic trends. **The threat to the United States is the persistent decline in the middle class's standard of living, a problem that is reshaping the social order that has been in place since World War II and that, if it continues, poses a threat to American power.**

American history was always filled with the assumption that upward mobility was possible. The Midwest and West opened land that could be exploited, and the massive industrialization in the late 19th and early 20th centuries opened opportunities. There was a systemic expectation of upward mobility built into American culture and reality.

GEORGE FRIEDMAN

A large body of research shows that when overall uncertainty increases, GDP falls. Companies invest less, trade less, and hire fewer people. Consumers spend less.

GEOFF COLVIN

As humans, we crave knowing what is going on and why, as surely as we depend on the rising and setting of the sun, the tide going out and returning, and oxygen filling the air. And when universal expectations of life-long employment and comfortable retirement seemingly vanish, challenging our known paradigm, we are emotionally unnerved—and understandably so. Yet as we struggle to discern the causes of various outlier events, we routinely reach for the simplest and singlest of answers. This search for simplicity solely to resolve some emotional anxiety misses the truth of the moment and robs us of the more complex answer. The simplistic answer, when followed to its logical conclusion, can often lead us to future behavior resulting in precisely the outcome we were trying to avoid.

Many economists would have us believe that markets (financial markets, job markets, etc.) exist in equilibrium: they behave according to rational, unremarkable, and efficient self-adjusting models. This does not take into account the irrational element of human behavior or the fact that some markets, including economic and job markets, live in a critical state of nonequilibrium. They are always on the edge of instability. Yet nonequilibrium markets generally act like equilibrium markets—until they don't. Then—*bang*—things seem to spiral out of control. These events seem abnormal and chaotic but are actually quite logical and routine, albeit somewhat irregular in their frequency.

While it would be all too easy to point to one root cause as an explanation for the tough job market we find ourselves in, the truth is that it is much more complex than that. I have, however, pointed to areas that have made our career path more complex. Just remember that no one contributing factor is in and of itself the sole cause of our job woes. Anyone who claims otherwise is either a charlatan or naïve, whether they prognosticate with genuinely good intentions or not. I highly recommend reading *Ubiquity: Why Catastrophes Happen*, by Mark Buchanan, in order to understand the states of equilibrium and nonequilibrium and how the latter live in a constant critical state (on the edge of radical change), prone to wild swings and catastrophes that are unpredictable in timing, but virtually certain to occur at some point in time. Although our economy and job markets have reflected a seeming calm on the surface for several decades, an outsized event like the economic crisis of 2008 has served to jolt us from our slumber.

PART 2

Stop the Education Madness!

The cost of college tuition has risen faster than nearly any other good or service in America for more than three decades. The average student loan borrower walks away almost $27,000 in debt for an undergraduate degree. Student loan debt has outpaced credit card debt in this country. These eye-popping prices have inspired a raging debate over whether college is really worth the money anymore.

ANYA KAMENETZ

Dramatically increasing tuition costs, ballooning student loan debt, the rise of alternatives to traditional colleges, increasing scrutiny of a profession's wages, the failure of a public high school system to prepare students for college, and a less certain job market are driving skepticism about the value of a public or private university education. Many state legislatures are reducing the amount of funding they provide to public colleges, further exacerbating the situation. Many college-age students are instead choosing to go to a technical college, community college, or simply trying to enter the job market out of high school. And it's not just students and parents who are starting to be skeptical of colleges and universities; now employers are jumping on the skepticism bandwagon. While GPAs have increased dramatically in recent years, according to a 2010 study by the Association of American Colleges and Universities, confidence among employers in GPAs has dropped to 25%. And with the number of A's awarded to students tripling since 1940, employers are starting to demand something be done. Some are experimenting with post-college testing to see how much knowledge the student has retained. Employers are also interested in the critical thinking skills of new hires given the ambiguous, ever-changing business environment with its faster-changing business cycles.

6

Out of Control Tuition

Tuition and fees growth have outpaced even the ginormous rise in medical/healthcare costs and cost of living (which have themselves been growing dramatically since the early 1990s), and the pace shows no signs of slowing. It is quite the opposite, an acceleration of inflation speed (see Figure 12).

Figure 12. Source: Doug Short, Advisor Perspectives

Not only have tuition and fees grown, total spending by universities has tripled between 1975 and 2005. Dur-

43

ing that same time, the student-to-teacher ratio has remained constant around 15 or 16 to 1. The increase in spending, rather than paying for more instructors, has gone to pay for more administrators. During the time period in question, the student-to-administrator ratio skyrocketed from 84 to 1 to 50 to 1, according to The Delta Cost Project (2010). While faculty ranks grew by about 50%, mirroring the increase in students, the number of administrators and administrative assistants grew by 84% and 240%, respectively. I recognize that many university presidents would say that the task of administering higher education has gotten more complex. But nearly a 70% overall increase in administration-to-student ratio, with virtually no change in teacher-to-student ratio, seems a bit excessive, especially with many universities complaining about tight budgets.

Surprisingly, given the immense amount of money coming through the door, universities are feeling the financial squeeze, largely because of competition for enrolling new students. According to *Inside Higher Ed's* 2017 survey, 56% of colleges failed to meet their 2016 enrollment goals. Colleges are trying to reverse this trend by recruiting more international students, transfer students, out-of-state students and "full-pay" students. The need for students who pay full price has led some colleges to accept applicants because they are "full-pay" students and rejecting others who aren't, simply on that basis and even when there are enrollment vacancies. Twenty-nine percent of college admissions directors admit to trying to poach students who have already committed to another college, even after the May 1st deadline.

There is a growing payola problem with international students from emerging markets paying to have their applications embellished so that colleges desperate for growing enrollment will accept them. In September 2013, the Assembly of the National Association for College Admission Counseling (NACAC) voted overwhelmingly to lift the ban on using commission incentivized agents to place international students at US universities. While we will wait to see how this plays out, I foresee international admission agents pursuing bonuses without regard to submitting quality candidates to universities as an unintended consequence of this strategy. And if that happens, the overall credibility of colleges will suffer even more and degrees from those institutions will carry less and less weight.

7

University Debt Bubble

The increase in student loan debt in the last two decades has far outstripped growth in nearly every other industry, including healthcare (but excluding tobacco and cigarettes, oddly enough). This debt places an undue burden on most graduating students. And to top it off, most of the increase in tuition has gone to pay for additional administration, not teachers. With 41 states decreasing their level of public college funding starting in 2008, federal grants decreasing, and the fact that more students question the wisdom of taking on significant amounts of student loan debt at a time when economic uncertainty persists, universities have less pricing power when it comes to raising tuition according to The Delta Cost Project. According to Moody's Investor Service, 72% of four-year public universities are seeing flat or declining net tuition, and with 80% of students attending public universities or colleges that are receiving less state funding, finances will be tight. While the Great Recession initially drove unemployed workers to go back to school, the continued economic malaise is driving them away due to price sensitivity, questioning the value of higher education, and their taking part-time, lower-paying jobs that won't afford them the money to get more education. One thing is for sure, college institutions without a clearly defined niche or unique value proposition to offer students will struggle most.

One of the dirty little secrets of college debt is that it is the only kind of debt that cannot be discharged under bankruptcy, so many lenders have relaxed their standards over the years, assured that they will get their money eventually. The staggering levels of student loan debt (compare the average amount of $9,450 in 1993 to a whopping $34,000 in 2017) has a negative impact on the overall economy. These new graduates have less discretionary income to spend. And over two-thirds of graduating students have debt equivalent to 60% of their average annual income, a crushing financial weight they must bear.

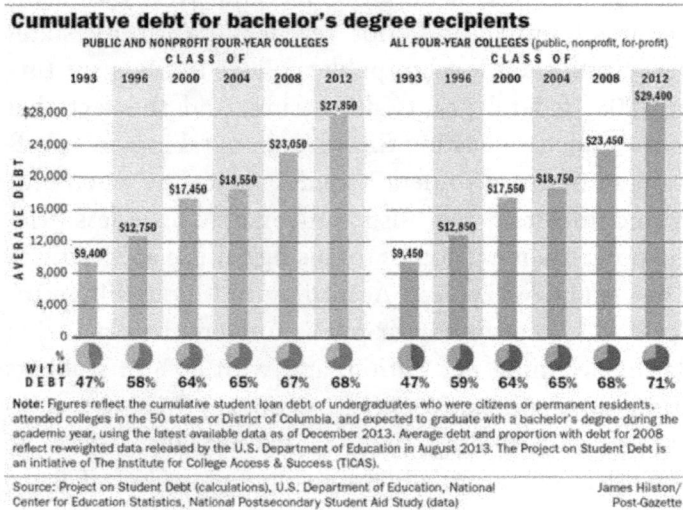

Cumulative debt for bachelor's degree recipients

	PUBLIC AND NONPROFIT FOUR-YEAR COLLEGES CLASS OF						ALL FOUR-YEAR COLLEGES (public, nonprofit, for-profit) CLASS OF					
	1993	1996	2000	2004	2008	2012	1993	1996	2000	2004	2008	2012
Average debt	$9,400	$12,750	$17,450	$18,550	$23,050	$27,850	$9,450	$12,850	$17,550	$18,750	$23,450	$29,400
% WITH DEBT	47%	58%	64%	65%	67%	68%	47%	59%	64%	65%	68%	71%

Note: Figures reflect the cumulative student loan debt of undergraduates who were citizens or permanent residents, attended colleges in the 50 states or District of Columbia, and expected to graduate with a bachelor's degree during the academic year, using the latest available data as of December 2013. Average debt and proportion with debt for 2008 reflect re-weighted data released by the U.S. Department of Education in August 2013. The Project on Student Debt is an initiative of The Institute for College Access & Success (TICAS).

Source: Project on Student Debt (calculations), U.S. Department of Education, National Center for Education Statistics, National Postsecondary Student Aid Study (data)

James Hilston/ Post-Gazette

Figure 13. Source: Copyright *Pittsburgh Post-Gazette*, 2014, all rights reserved. Reprinted with permission.

Even more disturbing than the growth rate of student debt is the delinquency rate (see Figure 14). This does not bode well for future generations that have no way to pay off student loans and no way to discharge the debt via bankruptcy. This is a ticking time bomb the government will be forced to deal with some day.

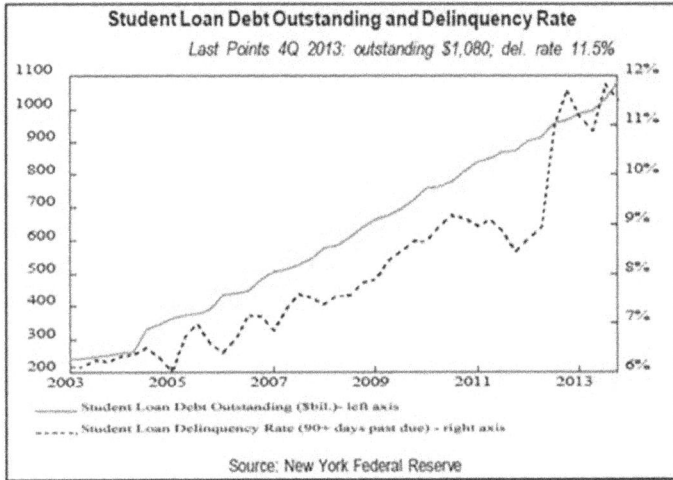

Figure 14. Source: Federal Reserve Bank of New York Consumer Credit Panel / Equifax.

If you have no student loan debt, consider yourself extremely fortunate! Be sure to carefully count the cost of accumulating student loan debt in the future. Just getting a degree isn't what it used to be. It needs to be a degree with genuinely high earning potential, based on actual historical data, not what your mother's sister's next-door neighbor heard. Make your decision after studying information from multiple credible sources. As a general rule, degrees in STEM (science, technology, engineering, and mathematics) will be in high demand for the foreseeable future.

Do not despair if you have a large student loan balance already. What's done is done, and no amount of regret will allow you to travel back in time and change those decisions. Here are a few tips on reducing student loan debt:

1. Be skeptical of programs that offer to substantially reduce your loans; there are scams out there. Congress has failed to pass a bill that would have allowed federal student loans to be refinanced at lower interest rates.
2. Pay as much as you can in order to reduce the principal balance sooner rather than later. The longer you wait to take care of debt, the more interest you will pay.
3. If you can't meet the minimum payments, don't panic; just pay what you can pay and communicate with your loan servicer about your financial challenges. Most of the time, you can apply for a temporary reprieve from payments or a lower monthly payment. Just remember that whatever interest you don't pay during these reprieves will be added to the loan balance, so only take advantage of them if you absolutely need to.
4. If you pay more than the minimum monthly payment, make sure to ask your loan servicer to apply the overpayment to principal, not just toward future minimum payments.
5. If you work for a non-profit, government, or other public service organization, apply for the Public Service Loan Forgiveness program. And if you are a teacher in a disadvantaged area, apply for the Teacher Loan Forgiveness program. But keep in mind that these jobs are generally lower pay and it takes a long time to qualify for the loan forgiveness programs. If you can pay it off more quickly

yourself, it may be worthwhile because you will be paying less interest.

6. Often you can receive a 0.25% reduction in interest by paying on time or signing up for automatic payments.

7. While it is always good to consult a tax adviser, usually you can deduct student loan interest on your federal and/or state income taxes.

8

Rise of the Technical College and Non-traditional Learning

Graduates of a local job-training program are scarfed up as soon as they finish.

DARLENE MILLER, CEO OF PERMAC INDUSTRIES, A 95-YEAR-OLD ELECTRONICS CONNECTOR MANUFACTURER

Not only do universities face pressure to explain their return on investment, they face stiff competition from new entrants to the education market. Technical colleges are adapting and growing rapidly, taking market share away from traditional institutions. If that weren't enough, many other companies selling nontraditional learning opportunities have sprouted, seemingly overnight. They mostly rely on new delivery technologies to keep their overhead costs low and in some cases offer a superior product for less money.

Not only are technical colleges better suited to some students' pocketbooks or their interests, many businesses, especially in manufacturing, are clamoring for technical colleges to educate young professionals in a way that universities are not set up to do. There are significant job opportunities in trades (plumbing, electrical, etc.) and skilled manufacturing where there is high demand but not enough trained workers. And businesses are partnering with technical colleges, government economic development departments, and chambers of commerce to train students for specific jobs the manufacturers need. Attending a technical college with one of these programs can virtually assure someone a high-paying job with much lower tuition and low-to-no student loan debt. Plus, the opportunities to apprentice for a trade job are many. Most trades simply have more need than there are applicants. Now, the hours for tradesmen aren't usually that great (nights and weekends), but there is great pay and stability. The key in any of these decisions is to understand that there are always tradeoffs, pros and cons. While going to a technical college may offer a good paying job, it may come with weird hours or less flexibility. And while choosing not to attend a traditional college may afford flexibility to chart your own course, charting your own course through a myriad of options can be daunting in and of itself.

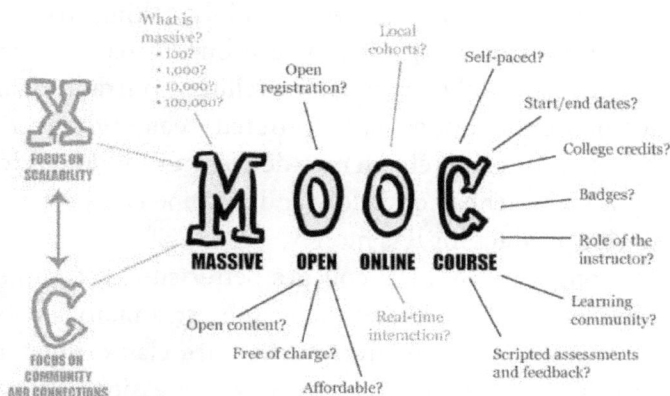

Figure 15. Source: Mathieu Plourde © 2013 https://www.flickr.com/photos/mathplourde/8620174342/sizes/l/in/photostream/

MOOCs (Massive Open Online Courses) are online courses offering unlimited participation and are generally free to attend; although some have minimal fees for attendance or for specific certification. Some are even suggesting that MOOCs will allow students to attain something similar to a business degree at significantly lower or no cost. The potential downsides are the lack of valuable human interaction and critical conversation with a professor and peers and quality and veracity of subject matter.

With the advent of MOOC-based institutions like Coursera, Udacity, edX, Udemy, and Khan Academy adding more competitive pressure to the traditional educational model of formal higher education, university presidents should be worried about their future enrollment numbers. While I am not proclaiming the end of traditional universities, universities of the future will have to prove their value (engagement in course material, live in-person debate, higher course completion rates, etc.) in order to justify to high school seniors and their parents the increasing costs of professors and large campuses. I don't believe traditional colleges will be able to increase their tuition nearly as much as they have in the last two decades. MOOCs will have a lasting impact in our education, not by destroying traditional universities but by causing them to adapt due to this competitive pressure. We will have different choices to make about furthering our education post-high-school. MOOCs are the latest entrant to the field, but soon there may be other choices beyond MOOCs. The landscape will continue to change as technology advances. So we must remain open to new ways of learning that are more relevant to the particular career we are pursuing.

Another form of nontraditional learning is studying internationally, which can help broaden our narrow "home country" bias and myopic focus. According to the website "100,000 Strong in the Americas," studying abroad can increase our regional prosperity. "Two trend lines inform the importance of study abroad: the Americas now can produce more petroleum-based energy than the Middle East, offering a future of energy self-sufficiency if we can come together in a constructive way. Secondly, by 2060, the population of the Americas is expected to be as great as that of China. Against this future landscape, study abroad throughout the U.S., Canada, Latin America, and the Caribbean will deepen relationships across the Hemisphere, enabling young people to understand and navigate the rich tapestry of values and culture we share. These students will lead the process of greater commercial and social integration key to our region's long term security and prosperity." For those of us in the US, this future provides a ray of hope for our careers amidst the upheaval we currently face.

9

Show Me the Money, Professor Practitioner

Many of the new high-paying jobs require the in-demand skills that typically come from learning from practitioners rather than academics. And at the risk of sounding like I despise research (which I don't), we don't have enough professors who are current, up-to-date practitioners in their field. Even those who are currently working in their field often have a dated viewpoint of the profession and are not in touch with critical changes that are happening in real time. While we do need researchers, higher education has far too high a percentage of professors who haven't been a practitioner in years, maybe even decades. This is an acute problem in many disciplines across higher education that are being taught on a theoretical level, rather than from practical, current experience in today's environment. Since I come from a business school background, I will use this to illustrate my point. While some subjects like accounting and finance change slowly, subjects like human resources, digital marketing, public relations, and economics are undergoing tectonic technological shifts, and most professors are simply not equipped to teach the latest methods. There are many websites that review professors independently of the university itself. These will help students and parents discern which professor is best suited to a student's needs. Whereas the education system used to be cookie cutter with large lecture halls being filled with hundreds or thousands of students at a time, the university of the future will require professors to become more and more specialized, tailoring their instruction for each student.

And in the name of all that is holy, please consider the wages of a particular profession before you select that degree plan. Don't just take the opinion of a professor, guidance counselor, parent, or someone else simply at face value. Talk to someone who is currently practicing (successfully, I might add) in your desired field and learn about the pay, working conditions, typical culture, etc. This sounds so simple and elementary, but you would be shocked to know how few people follow this prescription. It is not that you should never choose a lower-paying profession or one with drawbacks such as lousy hours. You have to weigh your sense of calling to a particular vocation as well. But you should be making an informed choice, unbiased by the school you are attending (which has a strong self-interest in selling you a degree plan at their school). Some guidance counselors, parents, or friends are more knowledgeable and impartial than others, but by and large, advisors could do a better job at preparing our high school graduates for the next step. And students can be just as guilty in assuming that other adults are knowledgeable enough about the current environment to map out their entire career. Perhaps that was the case several generations ago, but it is all up to us now. So stop complaining about things and embrace the responsibility. If you do, you will be well on your way toward a successful (not necessarily a secure or safe) career.

10

Progressive Education Has Failed Us

Not only are our universities falling short in achieving the career aspirations of graduates, but our nation's public school system isn't preparing most for college, further complicating things. And it isn't for lack of increased funding as many in the media, politics, and education would have you believe, Even after adjusting for inflation, the US public schools have increased the amount spent per child by 206% since 1971, yet math and reading achievement has remained flat during the same period of time.[3] Yet, we continue to hear that we need to spend more on education . . . for the children. Forgive me if I seem skeptical. I am all for education, but why spend more on a system that is clearly broken, rewards tenured teachers who don't teach well, and gives lip service to how much we are doing to make things better. Clearly, there is too much political power involved to do what's right for our children. Much of this is documented in the documentary *Waiting for Superman*, a film I highly recommend.

Add to this the fact that in the early 1900s, the US discarded a time-tested and well-performing method of education, the "classical" method, and replaced it with a "progressive" method of education. The key distinction between the two is that the aim of the progressive style is to create compliant citizens and factory workers who complete rote learning, obey the law, pay their taxes, and otherwise be compliant to their government, company, etc. The hallmark of the classical style is to create independent thinkers and lifelong learners who love reason and logic and can debate and speak eloquently about what they believe.

Progressive education also fundamentally transfers the responsibility of a child's education from the parents to the state. Parents have willingly handed over oversight of what schools are teaching their children, seeing formal education as a substitute for rather than an addition to taking time to teach them at home. To reverse this trend, there is renewed interest in the classical methodology of education in general. And while there is a Classical Christian movement afoot today, the classical method of education comes from ancient Greece and Rome which of course pre-date Christianity. The classical method is superior and needs serious consideration if we are to prepare our students for college and beyond. While I am not ready to wave the white flag of surrender just yet, I think there is such a strong political interest in keeping the status quo of our public school system that there is little hope of reforming them at present. I'm talking about resistance to performance based measurement for teachers, tenure without accountability, absolute resistance on pay/benefits, all backed by the deep pockets of the unions. The system is set up to protect teachers at the expense of the best interests of students. And before you start hatin' on me, consider that my mother was a special education teacher and my wife was a music teacher in the public school system for many years. I have respect for those public school teachers who do have the best interests of their students at heart.

What is increasingly needed to succeed in any career are the nontraditional and adaptable skills and experiences that the monolith of progressive education rarely provides. Skills like emotional intelligence, creative thinking, self-awareness, synthesization of disparate concepts, and adaptability to different industries, disciplines, and cultures are desperately needed in planning today's careers. Traditional clerical and mid-level management jobs are going the way of the buggy whip, and how we adapt to this changing climate will determine the fate of a generation of job seekers. The great news is that even though a good-paying blue- or white-collar job is not as common as it once was, we live in an age where there is more choice than ever before. It is just scarier because it isn't as easy to find the career path where you fit.

11

Wrap-up: Is College Relevant Anymore?

I refer to these as micro colleges. By 2030, the average person entering the workforce had better plan to reboot their career six times throughout their working life. This type of training will become very popular.

A SENIOR FUTURIST AND STRATEGIC FORESIGHT CONSULTANT

Perhaps a college education is still needed for many of us, but with skyrocketing costs (1,134% increase since 1978) and a growing multitude of alternatives, now more than ever before, we are forced to carefully weigh the return on investment of a college degree. If we chose not to count those costs and blindly accept that there is a strong return on investment, as previous generations have, most of us will be sorely mistaken, caught up in the exploding debt of a deadly assumption. Nontraditional learning options have increased in recent years with more change and disruption to follow; as with any of these choices, we will need to wisely select the best path for ourselves, one that is tailored to our needs and desires. On top of all of these challenges with higher education, our progressive educational philosophy falls woefully short of preparing our high school seniors for college. We will need to seriously consider alternative options for our children's elementary, middle, and high school learning if they are to be prepared for the onslaught of change after high school.

WARNING!

The advice I give in this book is relevant a vast majority of the time, but there will always be exceptions. So if you find yourself in a situation that seems like an exception given other information you have, you might be right.

PART 3

Embrace Becoming Generation Flux

The worst thing that happens to you could be the best thing that happens to you if you don't let it get the best of you.

WILL ROGERS

Are you stressed after reading the first two sections of this book? Or were you already stressed before reading this book, having lost a job or fearing your job being replaced by technology? Maybe you know someone going through this unfortunate job situation. Or perhaps you simply fear the unknown. From personal experience, these are normal emotions to feel given the circumstance.

But the rest of this book will do you no good if you don't find a way to rid your career and life of fear. With all of us at some point having to wrestle with negative thoughts, it can be tough to get in the right mindset to succeed in challenging times, but in order to embrace becoming generation flux, we must be in the right mindset or risk derailing our career. If we are not careful, our mind can play tricks on us making us read too much into observations of various career situations.

Consider some of the following questions you or others you know might have asked yourself:

- Why did they let me go? It must mean that I am not valued.
- The company seems to be in trouble. Will I be let go next?
- Are my outdated skills going to lead to lifelong low wages?
- Will I ever be employed again?
- Why won't the hiring manager call me back?
- Did I say something wrong in the interview?

And on and on our minds race with negative emotions and implications drawn from limited knowledge of various circumstances ... unless we chose to stop those thoughts and replace them with others that are more positive. If this is something you struggle with, please pick up a copy of my friend Christopher Paul Elliott's book *ThoughtShredder*. His easy-to-follow process will help you rid yourself of negative thoughts that will hold you back from reaping the benefits of the rest of this book. Part 3 will illuminate the changes taking place in the job market and how best to position yourself given the shifting sand.

12

Rise of the Generalist and Moneyball Workers

The new reality is multiple gigs, some of them
supershort, with constant pressure to learn
new things and adapt to new work situations,
and no guarantee that you'll stay in a single
industry. It can be daunting. It can be
exhausting. It can also be exhilarating.

ROBERT SAFIAN

One of the hardest things about finding a job is that
all of the stars (pay, timing, education, fit, etc.) need to
align at the same time in order for there to be accep-
tance of a job offer. There are so many different variables in play, and they all have to align near perfectly.
That's what makes it so difficult as a job seeker. Instead,
our focus should be on how we can tailor the skills,
experiences, education, etc., to the job for which we
are applying. Since the varying combinations of job
description are growing dizzyingly complex, it is nearly
impossible to prepare the exact skills, experiences, education, etc., to accurately predict what a company will
need to hire in the future. We need to find the right
cultural fit of a position with less focus on whether we
have too little or too much experience. Usually education is a factor, but we shouldn't get too hung up on

having the exact degree or specialized certifications. Many HR professionals and hiring managers are looking for the elusive "purple squirrel." They draw up the job description and pick out the ideal qualifications. Then they wait for a cookie-cutter candidate who fills the exact profile (certain years of experience, specific kind of experience, and specific industry experience). The tendency is to totally gloss over many qualified candidates as a result. In fact, I would argue that candidates who are likely to be more creative, more innovative, and perhaps even better team players are more generalist in their skill set and experience than specialist.

Generalists are unique in their ability to pivot their career to a different job title/description. They have cross-functional experience in finance, marketing, accounting, human resources, economics, and business history, and they have experience in disparate industries (e-commerce, non-profit, publishing, consumer goods, etc.). But the current model that our universities teach and our organizations' HR departments stalwartly defend is one of becoming a specialist for ten, fifteen, or twenty years before you can lead in a generalist capacity. In the ambiguous competitive landscape we find ourselves in, the old HR hiring model has become an anchor around their organizations' neck. Employees in those organizations do not know how to adapt in their role to help their organization compete in this digital age.

This has implications for both job seeker and recruiter alike. Job seekers must realize the sand they are standing on is shifting, and that they need to broaden their skill set, adding generalist skills and experience to their tool belt. And we must not assume that our employer will help us with this. It is up to us to add those skills and experience. For recruiters, the sand is also shifting, and while most employers haven't awoken to the changes and the dramatic impact that will come, we must prepare now to learn how to find more generalists. They will be needed in increasing numbers, and organizations will realize this before there are enough generalist candidates available, so it will require savvy recruiters to locate and woo them.

> The winds of innovation have brought us unthinkable volumes of new data. Regardless of your business function or industry, data will play an increasingly larger role in everything you do in the future.
>
> JORDY LEISER

The bestselling book *Moneyball* and blockbuster movie of the same name have popularized the notion of a manager (Billy Beane) using statistical analysis (sabermetrics) to predict a baseball player's future performance. While Beane, himself once a baseball player, had been heavily scouted to play Major League Baseball, his performance did not live up to the hype. After leaving the game, he joined the staff of the Oakland Athletics and worked his way up the ladder to Assistant GM to Sandy Alderson who introduced him to sabermetrics. Alderson believed that a small-market team like the A's with a smaller budget than other teams could find hidden value in atypical performance indicators that other teams weren't even paying attention to. This could give them a performance edge, or at least level the field.

The ability of candidates to pore over disparate data sets and synthesize them into something useful for decision-making will be in high demand in the coming years and will separate the top performers from those that are average. The future of our digital world is to parse volumes of data sets in order to compete, and those of us who resist this will find ourselves falling further and further behind in our careers. The marketing Moneyball executive is using software to capture consumer behavior online and translating that into actionable directives for the team to tailor marketing messages for specific users' tastes, delighting customers by delivering what they want when they want it. The physician Moneyball executive is using software to analyze his patient outcomes compared to those of his competitors and using that to better his performance, since healthcare (read insurance companies) are moving toward a fee for performance system (and away from a fee for service model). He will let the data point out his errors, ignoring his gut instinct and humbling his ego to help patients. The role of Moneyball executive will allow us to tackle old problems with fresh, data-driven insights. Do not resist this wave of change; if you do, it WILL kill your career eventually.

13

The Fallacy of Fear

Fear is not real. It is a product of thoughts you create. Do not misunderstand me. Danger is very real. But fear is a choice.

FROM THE MOVIE *AFTER EARTH*

No excuses. Life is what you make it, and our career is no different. Let's choose to fight through whatever bad economy we're going through. Whether it is classified as a recession or depression matters less than our response to the situation. The prognosticators on TV tell us that the reason that it's hard to find a job is that the economy isn't great, and while there is some truth to that, it is up to us to figure out a way around that and determine what we need to do to persevere. The solution is not about making excuses.

A drowning man will even grab onto an alligator.

BOB CHRONISTER

When we're desperate, our survival instincts kick in. And we will have the tendency to grab hold of whatever job we can in order to avoid drowning financially and emotionally. We will even want to hang on to something that could kill or hurt us. We should be mindful of this not only in ourselves but in discerning others' motives. We must believe in what we are selling (ourselves), or we will not have good results. This may seem obvious, but far too often we allow self-doubt to creep into our minds, which leads to fear. Fear or desperation is a hard thing to hide in a job interview. I recognize that this can be hard when our confidence in our own abilities is shaken by an unexpected firing or layoff, but we must choose to maintain a certain level of confidence or risk bombing interview after interview (if we even get an interview). Fear is paralyzing and obvious to interviewers who are not fearful.

Ask yourself, "What is the most courageous thing I've ever done?" Most people's answer to that is that they can't think of anything or they think of something that isn't really that courageous. For me, I've been very fortunate. There have been several things that have been a crazy move for me. Moving to Green Bay, Wisconsin from Tulsa, Oklahoma was one of them. I have not been afraid to try different jobs and leap from one company to another after three or four years, even though some of those jumps have not worked out. Some might argue that those have been detrimental to my career, but I would argue just the opposite. They have been very beneficial (and painful), since I have learned so much from them. Compare this to most people, who have had the same job with the same company, or have been with the same company in different jobs throughout their career. Well, there's nothing inherently wrong or bad about that. They have experienced a lot of life also, but they haven't had those courageous experiences. So I challenge you to have more courageous experiences and take chances. Take risks—not stupid risks, but calculated risks. Some calculated career risks turn into career crashes. The key is to make experienced risks but even that doesn't guarantee safety. Even NASCAR drivers with twenty years of experience still crash every now and again, but they do learn from these situations and make them less often. Even if things don't always work out, we still have to keep trying and learning new things. Over time, we will get better at making sound decisions.

> When you grow up, you tend to get told that the world is the way it is and your life is just to live your life inside the world, try not to bash into the walls too much, try to have a nice family, have fun, save a little money. That's a very limited life. Life can be much broader, once you discover one simple fact, and that is that everything around you that you call life was made up by people that were no smarter than you. And you can change it, you can influence it, you can build your own things that other people can use. Once you learn that, you'll never be the same again.
>
> STEVE JOBS

This statement by Steve Jobs embodies the fear many of us face given this new level of career ambiguity and uncertainty. We want to play it safe, to be comfortable, and we think the opposite of comfort is chaos, but I submit that the opposite of comfort is *achievement*. The idea that we all choose either comfort or achievement when making life's decisions comes from a good friend of mine, Chris Busch, who runs LightQuest Media, and I think he is right on the money. We all chose some blend of both, but ultimately, we choose one more than the other, and for some of us dramatically so. Stop and think about that for a minute and ask yourself, "Do I choose comfort or achievement more?" While comfort is not all bad, we must wisely consider our choice given the current job market. If we chose too much comfort, this economy will likely relegate us to low wages and little opportunity for advancement. On the other hand, if we select too much achievement, we may miss enjoying life (time with friends and family, hobbies, leisure activities, etc.). I personally wrestle with this one but tend to fall a bit more on the achievement side; a strong work ethic paired with a desire to build, create, and grow things drives me to achievement.

Whereas previous generations had to face some unpredictability, current generations are facing unprecedented levels of instability. The bottom line is that we will need to have a bit more motivation on the achievement side of things than previous generations did if we are to succeed in our careers. But perceived comfort, security, and safety in a career is largely an illusion anyway. Choosing the most secure path is not nearly as satisfying of a journey. Herein lies the good news; if we choose to face and overcome the fear that we won't be comfortable if we take risks associated with achievement, there is truly limitless career potential. It just won't be given to us; we will have to create it. Wouldn't you rather live an eventful life filled with successes and failures, a life that is engaging and exhilarating, rather than a boring but stable life (that is, by the way, a dying model anyway)? What an exciting time to be living! It will only be boring and scary if you cling to the safety-and-comfort-focused career-planning model. I want to reach my death bed having lived a full life, having chased my dreams and having stood up to my fears. Even though I will have many battle scars, I never want to wonder what would've happened had I taken a risk.

14

Career Opportunity Costs

New companies—even industries—rise and fall faster than ever: Witness Apple, Facebook, and Amazon; witness Research in Motion, Blockbuster, and MySpace; witness the iPad and, yes, cloud computing. Accepted models for success are proving vulnerable, and pressure is building on giants like GE and Nokia, as their historic advantages of scale and efficiency run up against the benefits of agility and quick course corrections. Meanwhile, the bonds between employer and employee, and between brands and their customers, are more tenuous than ever.

ROBERT SAFIAN

There are various "career opportunity costs" associated with different career choices. An "opportunity cost" is defined by Investopedia as "The cost of an alternative that must be forgone in order to pursue a certain action. Put another way, it is the benefit you could have received by taking an alternative action." Investopedia gives an example that precisely fits this book. "The opportunity cost of going to college is the money you would have earned if you worked instead. On the one hand, you lose four years of salary while getting your degree; on the other hand, you hope to earn more during your career, thanks to your education, to offset the lost wages." As many of us have come to realize, this is not always the case, sadly.

The important thing to remember is that there is usually something we have to give up to get something else, and we need to weigh those trade-offs carefully. For too long, parents, teachers, students, and guidance counselors have assumed that getting a college education was worth the tuition and debt, as opposed to getting a job right out of high school. This assumption has proved devastating for many a career. I can't tell you how often I hear that someone has forty to one hundred thousand dollars in student loan debt only to find out that they can only get a minimum-wage retail job. Or even if they can get a job in their educational field, their starting salary is barely above minimum wage, and paying off their student loans will take them a lifetime. Yet no one bothered to help them understand the economic decision that must be part of the career and college discussion. While I am not blaming any one group, we all must take responsibility to prepare our students (or take responsibility ourselves if we are the student) to make sound economic decisions about our career.

There are also other different career considerations to weigh beside financial ones. Each of the following will affect pay, quality of life, hours, financial flexibility, geographic flexibility, and/or creativity in some way.

- Choosing whether to marry and at what age (in your 20s, 30s, 40s, etc.)
- Selecting large stable company vs. small entrepreneurial company
- Renting vs. owning a home

- Choosing whether to have children, and at what age
- Working in our hometown vs. moving to a different city, state, or country
- Living in city vs. country
- Leaving vs. staying in a job
- Getting into debt at young age
- Relocating to another city, state, or country for better opportunities.

Speaking of relocation, organizations only pay to relocate people who solve a very specific problem or have a very specific skill set. So I encourage you to widen your job search area (outside the city you are in), but I caution you in applying for a particular position unless you have a really specific skill set that is truly hard to find. This could end up being a time suck and ultimately a dead end if you aren't a candidate they can't easily find in their local market.

Deciding whether to stay or leave a job or company is one fraught with risk, indecision, and fear as there are opportunity costs to be weighed. And that hesitation is for good reason. But simple mathematics calculations show, pretty convincingly I might add, that lifetime earnings can be dramatically higher for those who change companies every couple of years than those who remain loyal and stay indefinitely. While the latter used to be the norm and was rewarded by companies with generous annual wage increases, it is increasingly becoming a noose around our neck, tightening the wage increases to around 1-3% per year. According to a USA Today survey, wage increases for 2012, 2013, and 2014 are flat, averaging around 3%.[4] Factor in inflation at

3+%, and many are going backward in wages, not to mention many people who took pay cuts more significant than 3% in order to retain their jobs. Scary times indeed.

But all is not lost; as Figure 16 depicts, wages can grow at a higher rate by switching companies or jobs. Notice I said CAN, not WILL. It's like with anything else, there is no guarantee of more money any more than there is a guarantee of that new employment working out. But without risk, there is no chance for greater reward.

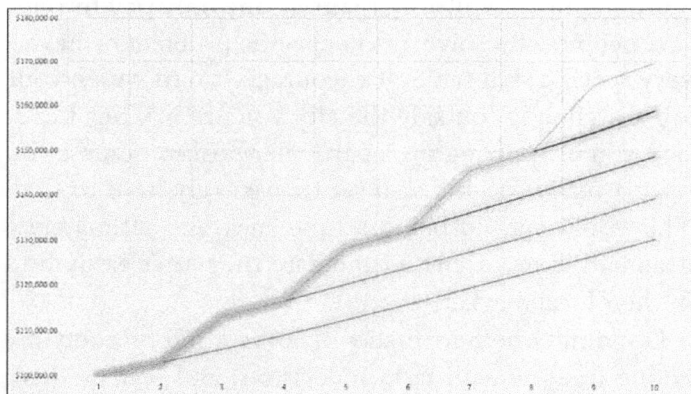

Figure 16. Source: Cameron Keng, Forbes Contributor

What this chart shows is a scenario where the average "loyal" worker gains 3% every year for ten years (the bottom light blue line), and a second scenario of multiple "potential" significant increases in salary by moving to a new company every couple of years for the same ten-year period. Clearly, this is a hypothetical scenario and unlikely to happen exactly like this, but the point is there is significantly more wage increase potential (a factor of 10-50% more) available by changing organizations. The old notion of employees feeling a sense of loyalty in exchange for modest increases in salary and an even more generous pension and lifelong healthcare benefits is being eroded to the point where it is swinging the other way toward short-term engagements at multiple companies.

Some may be afraid that having a resume with a different job every couple of years pegs them as a "job hopper", but the key difference is looking at what kinds of jobs the person left for the next job. If it was a scenario where there was little continuity among jobs, perhaps they are a "job hopper" who has poor work ethic. But this stigma is diminishing, especially as workers are being forced to change jobs more often in order to increase their earnings and responsibility, many of them with a strong work ethic and drive. And most companies are ill equipped for those who need rapid advancement and new opportunities every couple of years. Shorter employment is something many employers are also afraid of, but if they focus too much on this, they will pass over better quality talent who could accelerate their growth, albeit only for a couple of years. And in their place, they often settle for mediocre candidates they can hire cheaply and who will never want to leave. Is that really the kind of organization you want to work for?

15

Income Generation Redefined

With globalization as another powerful disruptor, per thought leader Thomas Friedman, U.S. jobs have now moved in three directions: up—requiring more education and technical knowledge, down—outsourced to history, and across—broken into job fragments, or short employment engagements, across the globe. Many people will not have annual salaries or set jobs in the traditional sense, but rather they'll generate income from leveraging and monetizing a combination of their physical assets and talents in an income-generation portfolio. They may rent a room in their house through airbnb, cook a dinner for a crowd that extends beyond their family advertised through feastly or Meal Sharing, run errands for others on TaskRabbit, drive an Uber or Lyft car, sell an idea through Quirky, market their goods through Etsy, sell clothing and accessories on Threadflip, and participate in short- and long-term freelance engagements through HireArt or Guru.

HEATHER MCGOWAN

Consider the fact that for the last fifty years, we have had the following career and income progression, one that was predictable if you followed the process set by previous generations. You created passive income and a generous lifetime pension if you followed the rules, went to college (then stopped formal learning), did what you were told, got promoted, and eventually retired in your sixties (see Figure 17).

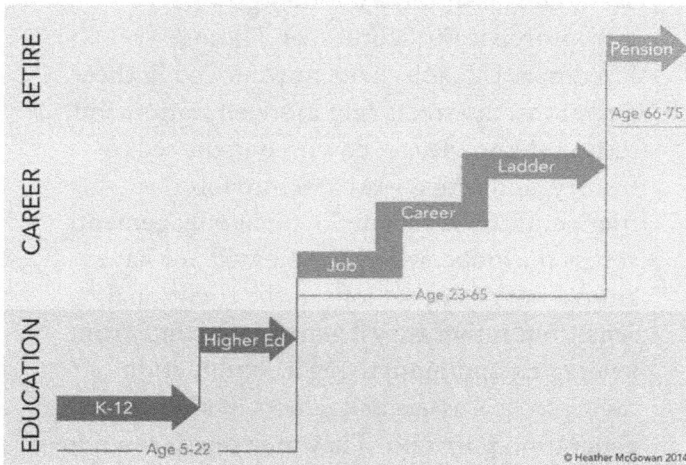

Figure 17

Now, with the level of change in our world accelerating at breakneck pace, this is what we must contend with (chart below). This is a picture of upward and backward progression, continual learning, rapid and relentless change, and taking control of how you earn income. So long retirement; you can expect to work into your seventies or eighties and must continually create and monetize assets (job, books, speaking, consulting, etc.), thus generating enough income to survive, not relying on a golden parachute pension.

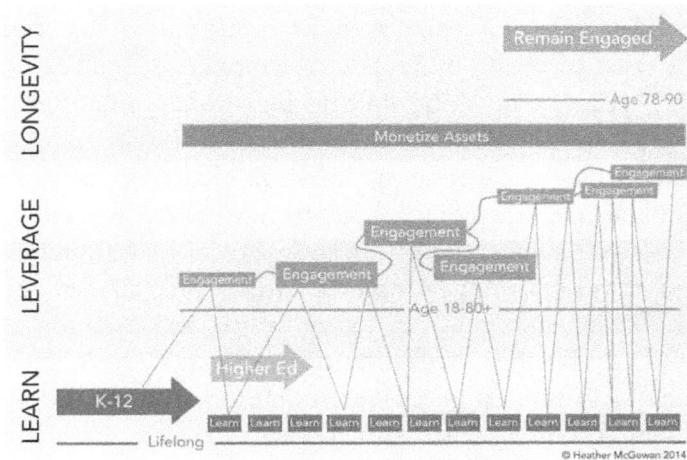

2000-2050: ERA OF INCOME GENERATION

Figure 18

Now, this new path of income generation lends itself to more of a reliance on shorter-term gigs to generate income rather than a lifelong career (whether with one or many companies) and less reliance on the safety net of pensions, savings, home equity, etc. While this picture of the future might sound terrifying, it is an opportunity to take more control of our career destiny by developing assets (physical products, services, connections, etc.) that can be weaved together and monetized over time, thus generating multiple streams of income. But make no mistake, we will have to be much more active in this than generations before.

There are really only two ways to make money. You can either sell your time to an organization, which will give you a fixed, guaranteed, reliable income (unless you get laid off), or you can sell something to generate your own variable, unguaranteed, unreliable income. Whichever single or combination of options is chosen

85

in the future, we should look at whatever money is coming into our bank account as cash flow that can be used to create more assets to monetize (see Figure 19). This is a key mind shift from previous generations, who looked at their job income as cash flow to pay for their lifestyle. Please don't miss this change in how we look at our income; it is vital to navigating the future. There are implications if we choose to spend our money on frivolous things (some of which isn't all bad) or invest in assets that can create future cash flow for us and our families. Accepting the fact that we will likely have less money in savings, home equity, and retirement accounts, which will create more gaps in income from time to time, should motivate us to use the income we have to create more monetizeable assets for future income harvesting.

JOBS vs. GIGS: INCOME + ASSETS

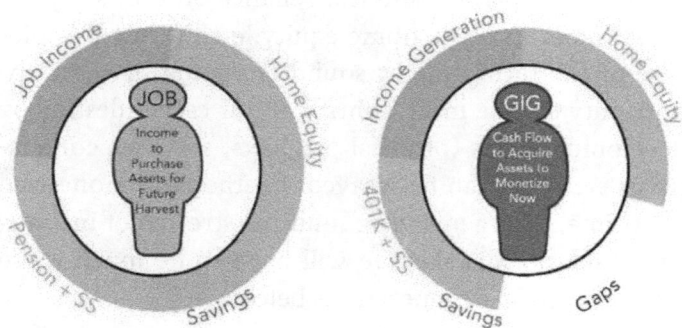

Figure 19. Source: Heather McGowan

The first income creation option (selling your time) is not as reliable as it was just a decade ago. You could say that there is a third option: being an independent contractor. In this scenario, you contract with a company for a period of time and number of hours, pay your own taxes, and go without the benefits of an employee. But this is really just a variation on the first option; the only difference is that you know your employment with the company has a defined length. Another growing alternative to option one is employee sharing. Multiple companies utilize the hours of a shared employee, since their need is less than the forty hours a week that would be required to find a quality employee solely for their company. This happens most frequently in accounting, HR, sales, and marketing, but may start happening in other fields. Just remember that this is more of the first model—selling your time. Others may choose to get a second or third job to create additional money; some may even have to work the second, third, or swing shift in their traditional job instead of first shift, both of which are also option one.

Most people will probably be more comfortable with one of these ways to make money than the other, but I would challenge you not to just do the one that you're comfortable with. Create multiple versions of option one if you are able. Then find something that can generate an additional revenue stream (option two) in addition to your option one stuff. We each have talents that could lend themselves to offering a product or service in our "after work hours." That way, we will not be solely dependent on our primary employer for income. This dynamic is changing quite a bit due to the muddle-through economy we find ourselves in. Many middle and lower class workers who cannot find traditional work are generating a revenue stream via freelancing work (independent contractor) to make ends meet. The US Bureau of Labor Statistics estimates freelancers, temps, and independent contractors will outnumber full-time workers by 2020, and those who embrace this new paradigm will be the winners. Those who don't may miss an opportunity to offset lower wages and fewer employment prospects.

Do you have the potential to create passive income that (over long periods of time and significant work—there is no get rich quick model) can work for you instead of you working for it? A benefit to having a side business is that you will learn things from that business that will help you in your primary job. I call this a "side hustle" to your day job. Focus on creating and selling some content (music, books, consumer good, etc.) that you can produce and sell over and over without your continued involvement in each sale. Of course, if you have success with your part-time hustle, don't give up your full-time job too quickly. A side hustle can take years, if not decades, to fully mature into a consistent, reliable revenue stream. While most employers want you to focus solely on your full-time job, I would argue that the employees' part-time hustle is actually beneficial to the full-time employers, as long as they don't interfere with one another and the employee continues to succeed at their primary job. The hustle makes the employee more creative and more understanding of how hard it is to be the owner. Also, they may apply something they learned from their hustle to their primary work and vice versa. It can create an innovative and creative feedback loop and cross-pollination. It's a symbiotic relationship.

But keep in mind that your employer may not consider your "side hustle" as symbiotic, and you may need to consult employment law to determine whether your employer may legally restrict your ability to participate in these kinds of activities. Typically larger employers don't care about it as long as it is done outside of work hours and it doesn't lower your productivity in your day job. Smaller employers tend to strongly discourage something on the side even if it is on your own time. And if you are contracted to work for an organization, then by all means read the agreement you signed to understand the potential ramifications of a "side hustle." Since most of us work in an "at-will employment" situation, what we do outside of work will have little or no negative impact on our day job. To be safe, you might want to restrict or limit the discussion of your "side hustle" with anyone at your day job (peer, supervisor, HR, etc.). And be sensitive to not working too many hours outside of work; this may unintentionally hurt your productivity or increase your tiredness. And be wary of MLM (multi-level marketing) and other pyramid schemes, Ponzi schemes, and get-rich-quick schemes when searching for a side hustle. These are very alluring but are ultimately distractions from finding something that fits who you are. Most of the time you spend an inordinate amount of time making other people money with little to show for it yourself.

As income generation has dramatically and fundamentally transformed the career landscape, ambiguity and fear have paralyzed many of us. We see a less secure career trajectory, wage, pension, etc. and want to hide our head in the sand until this season has passed. Yet, what we must do is embrace the new paradigm of income generation, realizing that there is actually more in our control than before. It just takes a more active role on our part to create multiple income streams, some traditional (employment) and some nontraditional (side hustle, content sales, product sales, job sharing, etc.). If we refuse to embrace this new paradigm and expect the government, employers, or someone else to fix the job market, we will be sorely disappointed.

16

Return of Frugality

With a major shift taking place in how we generate income, it would be a dereliction of duty not to consider how we spend our money. In order to survive a career in this challenging economy, we will probably need to be more frugal then we otherwise would like to be. Perhaps the last couple of generations didn't have to be as frugal as the economy now requires, but instead of bemoaning that, we should accept and embrace the positives of the situation.

Do you want a level of income to fit your lifestyle or a lifestyle to fit your income level?

You might think that this question doesn't make sense or represents circular logic, but my aim is get us to think differently about how we spend our money (which dictates how much income we need to earn). Would you rather wake up one day and realize that you are trapped in a "rat race," having accumulated so much debt that you must keep your job in your industry in your city, or would you rather intentionally choose a more moderate lifestyle (less expensive stuff, no or little debt), and have more flexibility in your career? I think we would all pick the latter, but most often we get started in a career and before we know it we are trying to keep up with the Joneses, piling on more debt by acquiescing to consumerism and bowing down to the god of a nicer home, clothes, school, vehicle, etc. I am not saying that we all have to live in poverty, but I am suggesting that we don't put the "income" cart before the "contentment" horse. We need to make an intentional choice on how we are going to live and not allow society to make that decision for us.

This causes us to be less consumerism minded; we really don't need as much stuff as we have or stuff as luxurious as we desire. Consider making large purchases, such as cars or appliances, from Craigslist instead of buying from a retail organization. I have personally participated in purchasing both a car and an appliance on Craigslist, and if you know what you're doing and are careful you can find good deals. Instead of financing that new vehicle purchase or lease, consider buying a used vehicle. Many people think that a vehicle is used up when it has 100,000 miles on it. While that used to be the case ten, fifteen, or twenty years ago, it is no longer the case for cars these days. Cars will legitimately last 250,000 to 300,000 miles if you take care of them by doing routine maintenance (oil changes, tires, brakes, muffler, struts, etc.). There is little maintenance on a good condition high-mileage vehicle unless there is something is that is abnormal about the car. But even then, if the engine and transmission are in good shape, there isn't much on a typical car that isn't worth fixing. Consider learning how to change your own oil in your vehicles, rotate your tires or other simple maintenance. While many would rather pay someone to do this rather than get their hands dirty, if you understand a bit more about car repair and maintenance, it is less likely a repair shop will take advantage of you by overcharging or recommending unnecessary repairs.

There is immense satisfaction in being able to fix things with our hands. These tasks have quickly become lost arts that many in Generations X and Y have no idea how to do. Sadly, our "Made in China or some other foreign country" consumerist culture has trained us to throw things away when they are broken because it is cheaper to replace the item than fix it. But if the cost is close, I suggest learning to repair things. I recently fixed the handle and plastic roller wheel on one of my luggage bags by finding the part on ebay, and there was a great sense of satisfaction from figuring out how to fix it. And when one of my car key fobs broke, I found the key fob shell on ebay, took it to the hardware store to get it cut, and swapped the electronic "guts" from one to the other. The whole thing cost me $20, when taking it to a dealership would've cost me $100-200. Perhaps you could consider gardening and/or canning. It is good physical exercise and generates fresher vegetables/fruits that you can eat yourself or sell at a local farmer's market to generate some income.

Maybe we need to secure clothing from Goodwill or other consignment store; while we may initially bristle at the idea, many of these organizations have good quality items. Now, they aren't designer clothing, but why waste extra money on stuff that doesn't matter in the long term? Consider shopping at Aldi or another discount grocery store. Some people like to engage in "extreme couponing" where they find tremendous savings on groceries (Google the term if you are curious), but I prefer not to have to hassle with that. My wife and I just shop at Aldi for most of our grocery purchases, since it is 40-50% cheaper there anyway. Pack a lunch for work instead of eating out. Now, we don't want to go to the extreme by becoming a miserly Scrooge, but if we are honest with ourselves, there is room to cut down on some expenses, which can help us increase our take-home pay. Take that extra money and save it for a time when you might find yourself unemployed or under-employed. How about coloring your own hair, ladies? Guys, have somebody give you a basic haircut with clippers.

Get out of debt and stay out. Pay cash for everything but a house. This may be hard, but it will help us weather a tough economic and employment climate that may persist for a decade or more. And it will allow us to be more generous towards others with the leftover money we would've used to service debt. We might think that frugality is stupid and below our station in life, but these choices are not really that bad compared to war, starvation, slavery, etc., and previous generations (mostly our grandparents and great-grandparents) had to be more frugal than they wanted to be too. Now we're facing similar times (not exactly the same but similar), so we should choose to become more frugal. There's really nothing wrong with it. It is just a practical part of our economy.

17

Action ≠ Intended Result

Correlation does not imply causation.

This statement is heard by every student who considers whether a career in academic research is right for them. Applying this rule to our lives means that simply because some action exists at the same time as success or failure does not mean that action caused the success or failure. Sometimes I wish the world were that simple, but it is not. We can do almost everything right in our career search and receive no job offers, and we can do almost everything wrong and receive multiple offers. Sometimes things are out of our control, as maddening as that can be. Our decision is whether or not we will persevere.

It is hard for me to accept that a particular action doesn't always get immediate results. Sometimes the result is delayed for weeks, months, or years. One of the great examples I can recall was when I was a used-car salesman at Chris Nikel Chrysler Jeep Dodge in Tulsa, Oklahoma, my hometown. There were times where I would go several days or even weeks without a selling a single vehicle. I would get frustrated because I didn't think that what I was doing was working, and maybe I needed to change what I was doing. In any situation, we need to remain open to the potential need to change what we're doing; but often times we can be doing the right thing but not getting the desired result. Sometimes that's just the way the cookie crumbles; sometimes life isn't fair. Sometimes we do things exactly the correct way, and the results don't line up with our actions in the way that we think they should. Sometimes we may be doing very little right and have all kinds of success and good performance. At the car dealership, I would see brand-new sales people who had no idea how to sell properly—couldn't sell their way out of a paper bag—falling into sales left and right. Needless to say, this was very frustrating and demoralizing, since I knew I was following the proper procedure. I learned (and am still learning) that direct action doesn't necessarily translate into direct performance. This doesn't mean we shouldn't attempt the proper action, but it just highlights the fact that there isn't always a direct correlation between action and performance.

This can be misleading when we are evaluating the performance of other people. We might think a particular person is doing a stellar job, when their performance is more of a function of the circumstances than their influence on the circumstances. This can cause them to look like they're doing a good job when they are really doing a terrible job. On the flip side, someone may be doing all the right things to succeed, but there are a number of things that just haven't paid off quite yet. Some strategies take longer to bring out results. I would encourage us all to be aware of this phenomenon in life and not get discouraged. Stick with what you know you're supposed to do, and things will work out right in the end. If you're reviewing someone else's performance (whether as a manager or peer), be very careful in drawing conclusions about causal relationships just from correlation of their actions and their performance. You have to make sure there's causality there. Recognize that it may take a long time to produce the desired results, especially if you're asking someone to come in and turn around a particular department or a company.

Everyone is dispensable but **some** are more dispensable than others.

We don't deserve our job. I don't intend to offend anybody, but the truth is that most of us don't deserve the jobs we have. There was some form of luck, serendipity, or blessing that resulted in securing our job. Maybe we were chosen for the internship because we knew somebody who opened the door for us that wouldn't have opened otherwise. Maybe we had an instant connection with the hiring manager during an interview. Maybe we were the better candidate from a choice of two mediocre candidates. Those events are what shape our careers, and the reality is and always has been, that is how we find jobs that help us grow and progress in our careers. The conventional wisdom (or better said, the wishful thinking) has been that if you just go to the right school and get a degree in your field, you'll find decent paying work. But this prescription just isn't going to cut it anymore. Rather, it will require a lot more effort on our part to find that career. It will be harder and more challenging, maybe even less pay, but if we seek meaningful work that fits with our motivational wiring, instead of the money, fame, and power most seek, we will succeed in ways that cannot be measured by traditional measures of success. This is something I struggle with. I often think that based on my skills, talents, and abilities, I should be the CEO of some department or company that is larger or more prestigious than the one I currently work for. I believe that I *could* have that job. I believe that I *should* have that job. Yet for whatever reason, my path and my journey is going in a different direction, and I have to be okay with the direction it's going.

I'm not saying that all is lost if you don't have the right connections to the right people, or that if you didn't go to the right school you can't have a good career. I'm just saying it is a lot harder to find your destined career niche, the one that holds meaningful, purposeful work designed just for you. If you are just looking for a job to make a good living and provide for your family, that job is almost nonexistent anymore. If those jobs do exist, they are on their way out, so you might as well assume that they are extinct. The sooner we figure that out and go in a different direction, the better off we'll be. Long gone are the days of the industrialist movement with their factory jobs and commonplace, manual labor. Manual-labor jobs are still out there, but you don't get paid much more than minimum wage, and you won't be middle class. We must accept the fact that we have to work much harder and smarter to find better paying and more meaningful work that we can be passionate and enthused about. While it is easier to find a job on the lower end of the pay scale, I can guarantee that it is much more meaningful and worthwhile to your circle of influence if you don't take the easy path. Your friends will see the fulfillment in your life and wonder what's different. I challenge and encourage you to pursue what you were designed for, what energizes you. And don't just do a job just because you're good at it. Passion and expertise are not always the same thing. Sometimes they are one and the same. You want to find a niche where they are the same, but just because you're good at math doesn't mean you should be an accountant. Many parents, college guidance counselors, grandparents, aunts and uncles, and other family members, well-meaning and well-intentioned though they are, set us off on the wrong journey or path by seeing something we're good at and pushing us in that direction.

18

Currency of Cultural Fit: Meaningful and Invaluable Work

Finding a job that is a good fit is as much about you selecting the right company as it is about them selecting the right candidate.

The real currency of employment is not experience and what's listed on a resume—it is whether there is a good cultural fit and whether the candidate has good emotional health (meaning they can work within a team environment). Sadly, many people hire based solely or primarily on experience, which can result in a dysfunctional chaotic team (if you can call it a team). I would always rather hire somebody with less experience and a good fit than a more experienced candidate who I know would be a bad fit. The person hired will need to work as part of a cohesive team of people. Hiring a disruptive superstar is much less desirable than a less talented or experienced person who can get along with others.

Half the battle of having a successful career is finding the right company that will give you opportunities to learn and will prepare you to advance to the next stage in your career (whether with that organization or some other one). While you may be looking for a particular

101

type of job in a particular type of industry, it comes down to knowing which organization will give you the right experience. This is not easy, but the more you can ask probing questions around that particular topic to understand the expertise that your potential boss and department have, the more you will understand if this organization will help you develop in your career. You don't want to be in an organization where you have more expertise and experience than they do. You don't want to be the smartest person in the room. Another bad position to be in is with an organization that isn't keeping up with the latest trends in their field or industry, since you may learn dated or bad habits that will lock you into a dead-end job/company and out of career growth. You want to be where you can expand your career, not in a place where you are being held back. The main thing to ask yourself about your organization is, "Is there a culture of learning?" If the answer is yes, then you are probably in a good place. If no, then find a way to learn and grow, so you can find another army to march with.

> The key to sustained employment will be to concentrate on the people skills that machines can't copy.
>
> GEORGE ANDERS

Risk is no longer a bad thing; we must accept the uncertain career outlook we now find ourselves in and embrace proactive, intelligent risk taking. The benefit of the tough economy is the fact that it forces us to pursue other avenues of work that we wouldn't have experienced if we were in a safe and secure career. The positive outcome of this is that it forces us to pursue something different rather than get stuck in a comfortable, safe, secure job that perhaps isn't all that you were designed for. In previous economic downturns just like our current malaise, many people were laid off and struggled to find comfortable, safe, replacement work. Even though it was challenging for all, some of them found their life's work, a more purposeful work that they may never have pursued had they not been laid off, downsized, or had their hours reduced. The circumstances forced them to examine things that were energizing and that they were passionate about to seek a career in something they strongly wanted to pursue. It pushed them out of their comfort zone without a secure job or career. It is a great opportunity for those of us who have been downsized, fired, or just can't find meaningful work. Focus on the work you do have and then begin to build a career around something you're passionate about. This might take five, ten, fifteen, or more years to get going, but it is worth pursuing. We all have a responsibility to seek out our desires, skills, and natural inclinations in areas that also drive, motivate, and energize us.

So often we focus on the job title, money, or position of power. We want to be at the top of the food chain, department, or company, and we really should be focusing on meaningful and valuable work that can't be outsourced to a foreign country or done by a machine. Finding your dream job is more about being content and faithful in your current job while you are building skills that will help you become a more valuable employee. It isn't about the fantasy of a magical job "somewhere out there" where they will pay us more money than we know what to do with, everyone will think we are awesome, and we'll get to do everything we enjoy and shun everything we hate. While there are jobs that are a better fit for us than others, we need to keep perspective in the situation and discern whether it is the best fit for the present time in our career. And finding work that cannot be outsourced to cheaper foreign labor or domestic machines is going to get increasingly difficult. The focus should be acquiring skills that will be valuable to many organizations, not just one, since that one organization could be caught up in a sea change and go out of business overnight. That is why it is super important to learn new skills ALL THE TIME, skills that are transferrable to another department, company, or industry. This point cannot be overstated. We all learn at some point in our career that things we are learning now may be obsolete in a few years. It is an unsettling thought, yes, but one that is exciting at the same time. Those who embrace change by shedding obsolete skills while learning new ones will be the winners, not those who bemoan change and long for the good ol' days.

19

Frustration:
Have You Given Up?

It's not you, it's me.

GEORGE COSTANZA

There are times in every career, mine included, when we wonder if we are stuck in a dead-end job or company. We may ask ourselves, "Should I stay, or should I leave my company or position?" This happens to all of us, no matter how engaged we are. Now, we have two options to pursue. We can give up and settle for the job we have, doing what we need to get by and please our boss, or we can choose to prepare ourselves for exiting the company at some point in the future. Did you catch that? I didn't say exit the company. I said prepare for exiting the company. And remember that we need to remain flexible in any job situation to understand the best time to leave.

There really are two main reasons why many of us, myself included, get frustrated early on in our careers. Number one is that we aren't happy with what we've already accomplished in our career. Maybe you just got married, and your spouse's job and career are going swimmingly. But yours isn't. Or in the midst of the daily grind, we get frustrated not looking at things from a higher point of view. I fall prey to this one at times, but when I step back and look at things in perspective, I recognize how much I really have accomplished and learned, resulting in personal and professional growth. Number two is that we want to get there now; we want to be in charge now. We want to have the responsibility now. We want success now. What we don't often realize is that it takes a lifetime over a long career to accomplish many of our goals. Subconsciously, we see what our parents or older professionals have accomplished and often gloss over how long and what it took to get where they are now. It doesn't help that the media tends to sensationalize the various people who do achieve wild success at a young age, like Mark Zuckerberg of Facebook fame. Maybe you do have the skills, abilities, and experience to do that now, but I would argue that you are likely not ready to handle that kind of power. Even if we are learning and becoming better leaders all along, it still takes a lifetime to mature. That perspective and understanding may make it easier for you to not want to be further in your career then you are.

It reveals a grave fallacy in the thinking of many (dare I say, the vast majority of) job seekers that entrepreneurship is seen as the escape from the 9-to-5 job working for "the man." Have you given up on your job search and want to become an entrepreneur? I certainly don't want to discourage people from entrepreneurship, but I think more people need to know about the risks. They need to reckon whether they are in a position to take on that risk. If you have a spouse and several children and you are the sole breadwinner of the family, I would stay working for someone else. Hopefully you can find something full time that will allow you to work on your business in the evenings and weekends. But remember that it will take at a minimum seven to ten years before you see even a dime of profit. That means you will be losing money for the first five to seven years. You need a significant a nest egg that you can invest in that business and then have a good business plan to be sure that it's going to return. Don't reach for education either as the sole solution to your job blues either. It is a costly solution and could make things worse (more debt and still no better job). It's like being an entrepreneur. Instead of investing everything in a degree or a full-time new business, it's better to bootstrap things. What incremental move (a single course, a single gig) can benefit you in the short term and lay the groundwork for long-term benefits?

I'm much too young to feel this damn old.

GARTH BROOKS

At a previous company, it got to the point where every time I went to the restroom, I rested my head against the wall above the urinal. This went on for several weeks, ultimately ending in employment separation. And I now tell myself that if I ever get to the place where I rest my head on the wall above the urinal several days or weeks in a row, it is time to find another company, department, or position to work with. If you are wondering if your job isn't the best fit for you, here are six signs according to Dr. Marla Gottschalk.

1. You feel lost.
2. You are in avoidance mode.
3. Your strengths aren't being tapped.

4. You feel disconnected.
5. You can't seem to complete anything.
6. You are entering self-blame mode.[5]

And if our employer chooses to terminate our job, what do we do then? This is a scary time in any career, and it requires perseverance, patience, and some luck. Recognize the fear, and don't let it turn into panic. That will kill your interviewing prospects, hireability, and dampen your overall mood. Here are some action steps to take immediately, in order of importance.

1. As stated before, don't panic! This is a traumatizing event, but panic leads to desperation. And desperation is noticeable to your interviewers even if you try to hide it. Don't go there. Now, I am not expecting that we are emotionless robots; we can be frustrated and sad, but resist depression. It will kill your hireability.
2. Focus on what you can control.
3. Proactively cut personal expenses, and do it before you have to. This is something I didn't do soon enough during a particularly long bout of unemployment. Think like a ruthless cost-cutting businessperson even if you have a severance package. Cut anything that is not essential. Some potential areas to look at: cable bill, eating out, cars with a loan/lease, and reducing any and all debts you can.
4. Can you survive on your spouse's income alone? Notice I didn't say live; I said survive. The answer to this question will determine how aggressive

your search has to be and how willing you should be to accept a job offer with lower pay. I have had to do this before as I am the primary breadwinner in my household. I recommend trying to avoid settling for a poor cultural fit with an organization and poor pay. I prefer to enjoy the work environment even if the pay sucks, but if both are poor and you have to, you have to. One in the hand is worth two in the bush.

5. Locate companies in ANY state (not just your own) in your specific line of work (the more specific the better), and apply for positions they have open. Focusing on your own city/state at the exclusion of other locations is a common mistake job seekers make. I personally learned this one the hard way.

6. Don't panic or become desperate. Focus on what you can control.

7. Call the top ten people in your network that are connected in your specific industry and ask them to help you spread the word, but don't expect that they will get you a job. Often, they can give advice and encouragement.

8. Locate organizations within your specific industry where there aren't any job postings and reach out to hiring managers with a pain letter pitch (see discussion about this later in the book).

9. Don't panic or become desperate. Focus on what you can control.

10. Depending on how much severance or unemployment income you have, you may need to look at getting an interim job to pay the bills. Mow lawns, do other odd jobs, work in retail, or anything else to keep money flowing in.

11. Rely on your closest friends and family for support
     and encouragement. Do not isolate yourself from
     people who care; just isolate yourself from people
     who are negative. This cannot be overstated or
     undervalued. Emotional well-being is vital to
     tackling the challenge of a job search these days.

Generally speaking, career counselors recommend that
we don't quit a job until we have another lined up,
unless there are truly dire circumstances (fraud or other
illegal behavior) NOT inconveniences (I can't stand my
boss, coworker, etc.). When you lose a job, it's obvious
that it is time to look for another one, but knowing
when to start looking for another job while you are currently employed is not that simple. The following are
three questions to ask yourself to know if you are ready
to start looking. You need to be able to answer yes to all
of these. You are ready when you say yes to three out of
three.

1. Am I leaving for the right reasons?
2. Am I prepared to leave in the right way?
3. Am I leaving at the right time?

The first question gets at the heart of the matter; have
I learned everything I need to in this role in order to
progress in my career? Maybe you believe your boss
sucks, but instead of complaining about that, perhaps
you need to do some self-examination to see what you
need to do to deserve a better boss. Maybe the reason
that you keep having bad bosses has to do more with

you than with them. Maybe you don't like your job or role, but if you leave and haven't gained what you need for the next chapter of your journey, you will inevitably be frustrated at the next job. You will be frustrated until you learn what you need to graduate to that next role.

The second question speaks to our motives for looking/leaving; will I give plenty of notice, or will I bail without notice because I am holding a grudge about something my employer did to wrong me? If the latter, let that stuff go before you start looking. And the third question asks if are there other factors to be considered that indicate that this isn't the best timing. Maybe you just got married, are having your first child, just moved into a new home, the health of your parent or grandparent is failing, or other factors too numerous to list here.

When we decide to leave, and if we were previously unwilling to challenge our boss or organization about something we strongly disagreed on, why would we air our dirty laundry during an exit interview? For some reason, people feel the need to unburden themselves during the exit interview, and this happens all too often. If we don't have the guts to tell our supervisor or peer something that frustrated us, then what gives us the right to air it to HR? It won't make the organization address that area of frustration after we leave; it will only mar our reputation after we leave. Let's keep that stuff to ourselves when we leave and leave on a good note. And when you leave an organization where you had a bad employment experience, don't be surprised if the next one doesn't work out quite the way you envisioned either. But if you are persistent, the next one will almost always be better even if only slightly. I can't explain why this happens, but I have seen this occur with me and countless others. I think what happens is that we are being tested to see if we will settle for our old job or one like it or if we will sacrifice for a better one.

20

Wrap-up: Embrace R&B

Generation Flux will be the ones successfully leading organizations, non-profit and for-profit alike, into the coming decades. Despite our nagging fears, soaring cost of living, stagnant wages, labor competition, exploding debt loads, and overall career complexity, we will choose courage and forge new careers across multiple industries and varied job titles. But with this faster pace of technological change, business cycles, and job position, we will need to embrace a "Recharge and Brain Breather" mindset. With so much career chaos swirling around us, we must recognize the vital need to take time away from work to rest and recharge. While this was an option before, in the future, it will be necessary if we don't want to feel run down or get sick all the time. The temptation is to do just the opposite, since we feel the pressure to perform and not get behind the competition. But wise workers will realize that in order to keep up with the pace of change and to stay innovative and creative (two highly important keys to success), we must have downtime. Think about it like this: working less is actually allowing us to be more productive during the times we are working.

PART 4

Hope in the Job-Seeking Trenches

Nostalgia is a natural human emotion, a survival mechanism that pushes people to avoid risk by applying what they've learned and relying on what's worked before. It's also about as useful as an appendix right now. When times seem uncertain, we instinctively become more conservative; we look to the past, to times that seem simpler, and we have the urge to re-create them. This impulse is as true for businesses as for people. But when the past has been blown away by new technology, by the ubiquitous and always-on global hypernetwork, beloved past practices may well be useless.

ROBERT SAFIAN

The one true constant in all of this is that those who continue to learn and acquire new skills will win in their career. Our mantra should be learn, relearn, repeat. We must refuse the urge to give up or pine for the past. Our minds can play tricks on us, leading us to long for an over-romanticized view of the past. This is only a mirage and will not save us from the present. In fact, repeating exactly what we used to do in the "glory days," will frequently result in a far more disastrous outcome. We must recognize our current situation and develop new strategies to deal with a rapidly evolving world. But we must not lose sight of the fact that there is hope for our career; despite the considerable challenges we face, things are far from apocalyptic. Part 4 will unpack practical action steps you can take during a job search and equip you with the strategies you need to chart the course of your career.

21

Why the Great Recession Is Good for Your Career

There are 80 million Baby Boomers set to retire over the next 5 to 7 years, and they're going to be replaced by 40 Million Generation Xers. That's two to one, so you'd better be developing your next generation now if you're going to be ready for that transition.

MICHAEL WHITE, CHAIRMAN, PRESIDENT & CEO OF THE DIRECT TV GROUP INC.

This should be quite the wakeup call for recruiters and HR professionals and encouraging to those of us who are Generation Xers. There will be a turnover in management like we haven't seen for a generation or two that will be an amazing opportunity for Generation Xers. Then they will have an opportunity to help Millennials transition into management in another fifteen years after that. So don't despair over the tough job market; there are always two sides to the coin. There is always opportunity, even in the darkest of times, just like there were companies started during the Great Depression. During times of contracted employment in some industries (those hit hardest by our current Great Recession), there is expanding employment in other industries that are better at supplying the increasing demand. Customers still need to purchase stuff. A 2009 study by Courtney Coile and Phillip B. Levine concludes that contrary to the popular belief that the recent Great Recession delayed retirements, it actually accelerated them. This means there is even more job demand, prime opportunity for the next generation ready to take on new roles and challenges.[6] It is up to us to seek out the organizations that are growing and/or losing retiring executives, all the while building adaptable and transferable skills in case that organization stumbles.

Figure 20

And there is evidence that in certain industries and for certain jobs, there is a growing unmet demand based on the average time to fill a position. At a national average of twenty-eight days to fill a position, the upward trajectory shows no sign of abating since the recession (see Figure 20). And according to the US Bureau of Labor Statistics, there are more jobs open now (6 million) largely unchanged for the last few years. Given the labor participation rate decline, it seems to indicate that some of these jobs are staying open longer or remaining unfilled. I smell opportunity here. There are other factors affecting this and many different explanations depending on your viewpoint, among them the search for the aforementioned imaginary purple squirrel candidate.

While I am not suggesting that those who are unemployed or underemployed should start their own company, here is a list of companies that started during the midst of the Great Depression and are still in existence today. Reviewing this list ought to give you encouragement and perspective that things aren't as bad as they might seem. It just goes to prove that innovation accelerates during times of economic challenge, and those who embrace change and innovate their careers will be the winners of this era.

General Foods, Bob's Big Boy, Gruman, GEICO, Macy's, Ricoh, Standard Brands, Smithfield Foods, Sony Music, Stater Brothers, Walt Disney Pictures, Colonial Life, Duracell, Earl Scheib, Fisher-Price, Krispy Kreme, Hostess Brands, Metro-Goldwyn-Mayer, Westin Hotels, Osco Drug, Pepperidge Farm, Polaroid Corporation, Allstate, Polaroid Eyewear, Bridgestone, Progressive Casualty Insurance, Clifton's Cafeteria, Putnam Investments, Porsche, Ray Ban, Swissair, Red Lion Hotels, Ritz-Carlton Hotel Company, Robert Hall, Advance Auto Parts, Saab, Ethan Allen Furniture, Sheraton Hotels and Resorts, Playtex, Stuckey's, Revlon, T. Rowe Price, Zippo, Volkswagen, E & J Gallo Winery,

Du–par's, Lacoste, Longs Drugs, Nissan Motors, Samsung, North American Van Lines, Rubbermaid, Ryder, Foster Farms, Warner Bros. Cartoons, Hewlett Packard, Peterbilt, Sara Lee Corporation, Latham & Watkins, Travelodge, Steak 'n Shake, Warburg Pincus, United Airlines, Wescom Credit, Day-Timer, Dairy Queen, Hasbro, Bank of Canada, McDonald's, Fujitsu, Sega, General Nutrition Centers, Kitchens of Sara Lee, Penguin Books, Raley's Supermarkets, Republic Pictures, and Tyson Foods

22

Four Career Phases

There remains a natural career progression even though the tougher job climate seeks to delay it.

1. At first, we till up the ground, plant seeds, and water. This represents the hard work for which we may not see much of a return in the early phases of our career, like getting a university degree, working more than one job, putting in extra hours, all during which time you are raising children, being involved with volunteer activities, friends, etc. This is a mentally and physically exhausting phase.
2. We start to see things grow and some of the crops have fruit. Our hard work is beginning to pay off, but there is still some instability and insecurity with our career.
3. We reap even more of the benefits of all our hard work. We are making a really good wage and a more comfortable station in life, yet it is easy to get too comfortable here and start to slack off or coast.
4. We make it to retirement or the waning years where we can give more of our time to volunteering as opposed to earlier because now we have more financial wealth.

Both phases 1 and 2 may take longer than they did in the past, but don't be discouraged. Keep your head down, keep working, keep pushing forward, and eventually you will breakthrough. But it is in that phase 1 where we tend to think that maybe the extra effort is not worth it. Maybe it is not working. The key is to not lose focus during those challenging times because if we persevere, eventually things will pay off. We must focus on how we're wired and seek the best thing for our career. Don't forget that much of the return on our effort comes through things other than money (health, relationships, contentment, etc.). The key to matriculating to phase 3 and 4 is to figure out how to learn as much about ourselves and what we enjoy as fast as is possible in order to begin to know what we want to be when we grow up. Now, there is always an element of continuing to learn who we are, and frankly what we do may need to morph in the future. But fundamentally, the question that needs to be answered is, how are we wired and how does that fit into the work world?

The quickest way to learn this is NOT to work for large companies like Google, McKinsey, Apple, or some other hot tech company right out of college. Some may think that given all of the uncertainty, larger organizations offer more stability and safety with better benefits and pay. Sometimes this is true and sometimes it isn't. If we do, we will likely get pigeonholed in one area or department, comfortable with a nice wage and accustomed to the accompanying lifestyle, all without learning much outside of our little bubble. The other option is a foggier path with many starts and stops, less guaranteed income, but superior experience and broader exposure. And we are able to learn more about ourselves, since we are closer to organizational problems and the solutions we can apply. In larger organizations, we are just too far away from the problem to make any real, direct impact ourselves. Working for many different smaller companies (for-profit and non-profit) in many different industries where we have more autonomy and exposure to more variety is a more accelerated career path no matter what our college guidance counselor or job fair recruiter tells us.

Starting to work for a large company first is like growing up in a small town and never traveling outside the city limits, while the latter option is like immersing yourself in many foreign cultures by spending time in those countries around the world. It's not that the first option is necessarily bad, but it does limit understanding and experience in exchange for perceived income stability. And if we want to work for a larger, established company later in our career, then we will be better prepared with a more robust skill set and a better understanding of ourselves in order to tackle those challenges more effectively. With all of that said, some larger and some smaller organizations will grow, and there is no right or wrong answer 100% of the time. The key is that our current economic period will be punctuated by higher perceived risk when the actual risk may be lesser, so choose the size of company wisely based on your personal situation.

23

What Tactics and
Which Careers?

The question we should be asking isn't, "what search tactic should I use?" (Although I would answer, "As many as are necessary and relevant given your industry, role, pay, location, etc.) The better question to ask is, "which tactic should I NOT use and which one should I start with first?" This allows us to decide which tactic will give us the largest impact for time spent. Prioritization is key when it comes to launching a job search strategy. Here are the results from a 2016 survey by recruiting authority Lou Adler:

Tactic Used to Secure Job	Internal Move or Networking	Job Ad
% Effectiveness	85%	15%

This survey holds with a 2012 Right Management survey of 46,000 Americans and Canadians. These numbers are averages and don't account for differences by industry. So experiment to see what works for your industry, then home in on the tactic that is the biggest return on your time. Otherwise, tons of time can be wasted on a job search.

	2012	2011	2010	2009	2008
Agency/ recruiter	14%	13%	10%	9%	12%
Direct approach	7%	7%	8%	8%	9%
Internet job board	25%	26%	24%	19%	19%
Newspaper/ periodical	1%	1%	2%	6%	7%
Networking	46%	45%	47%	48%	41%
Other	7%	8%	9%	12%	12%

Now, what is the best way to uncover these jobs? The answer to that is increasingly complex, since there are so many variables to consider. I would definitely start with networking/internal openings first and job boards second, since they have the highest chance for success. And while many advise us not to visit job boards, they still account for the second most effective way to land a job. We can't toss this one out as not valid. There are certainly many job boards out there; the key is to find the right niche ones. Here are a few to general job search sites to consider: Indeed.com and LinkedIn.com. Both of these can be setup to e-mail you search results based on specific geographic and keyword info you enter. Depending on the industry and pay range you are seeking, look for niche sites like Bigshoesnetwork.com, Cpgjobs.com, and Theladders.com. There are too many to list here, but the key is to take a targeted instead of a shotgun approach. Now, combine job boards with net-working (which I cover in a separate section shortly), and you have covered 81% of the most effective tactics to landing a job. Those are good odds.

Some career advisors promote the direct approach of using a "pain letter" to coax a company to create a job for you. This technique is advertised as a substitute for the job board or recruiter approach, but keep in mind that the effectiveness of this "direct approach" was only 8%. I still think there is merit to that approach, but I wouldn't spend more than 10% of my time on sending out cold letters/e-mails, even if they speak to the pain of the hiring manager. Instead, you could take the idea of a pain letter and apply it to cover letters and resumes to companies where you already have a connection (net-working approach). In general, I advise job seekers to use the percentages above to determine the proportion of hours they are committing to each technique.

You will need to customize and tailor your cover let-ter, resume, interview, and references given what you learn about each company AND each job. Don't blast resumes and cover letters at companies; it won't work. Trust me; I've tried. And remember the role of each of the following parts of the application process. While this may sound elementary, we too often lose sight of the process during the job search and think that the resume alone will get us the job.

- The goal of the cover letter and resume is to get an interview, not get you the job.
- The goal of the interview is to convince them that you want and can do the job.
- The goal of behavioral assessments and other tests is to understand if you will be a cultural fit. (There is nothing to do here, since you are who you are, and trying to fake these tests usually gets you disqualified.)
- The goal of references is to confirm or deny what has been learned throughout the entire process . . . call it the final double check.

And the same applies to choosing a career. Instead of searching for the needle in the haystack, perhaps we should burn some hay! Start eliminating careers and industries you know you won't like at all. Capture what you think you will love or are ambivalent about. Then start looking at the pay, supply/demand of applicants, and other intangibles (hours, culture, size of company) to refine your search. Recognize that this is not all science. It is some part art, and it might take a long journey to find "it." Then "it" may change, and you have to start all over. The key is to keep learning more about yourself and how you can fit that to what the marketplace wants.

So what are the toughest jobs to fill and thus have better than average potential career prospects? According to the 2013 Talent Shortage Survey compiled by Manpower Group, the top ten toughest jobs to fill are:

1. Skilled Trades
2. IT Staff

3. Sales Representatives
4. Engineers
5. Technicians
6. Drivers
7. Accounting & Finance Staff
8. Management/Executives
9. Production/Machine Operations
10. Office Support Staff

We cannot simply look at the list of toughest jobs to fill and randomly choose one if we want to be successful. We can't say that we only want to seek out larger employers over smaller ones. We must understand the pay, hours, size, etc., that accompany each opportunity. But at least we know where the demand for jobs currently is. Just know that this will change again and again. Nothing remains static. The Baby Boomers are about to retire from the workforce in droves, setting off a reaction that will escalate a shortage of certain talent, since most companies are not preparing for this massive handoff.

24

Cast a Smaller Net, Become a Pseudo-Insider, and Uncover Your Dream Job

If there is a job you really want, will you have the courage to potentially go backwards at a professional level in both responsibility and money because you really want to try it?

ALEX MALLEY

Some might think that a section on uncovering a dream job is the secret to winning the job lottery, but that would only be partially true. Searching for and finding your dream job is hard work; it takes years, sometimes five, ten, or fifteen years. And as Alex Malley and Heather McGowan point out, our career path and income may move forward, backward, up, down, starting and stopping, yet we must choose to face this new reality with courage. Keep in mind that sometimes we will be forced to go sideways through something outside of our control, but other times may call for choosing to go backward or sideways in order to go forward in the future. This may seem counterintuitive and cause frustration, but it may be just what your career needs to succeed. Over time and using the following ideas, you too can find that dream job. The key is not giving up!

- Identify organizations that share your personal values, focusing on cultural fit, whether or not they have a relevant job opening posted currently.
- Find and target industry-specific job sites; don't waste your time with Monster, CareerBuilder, and the like.
- Research salary ranges in the local market; pay is very different in Omaha, Nebraska, versus San Diego, California.
- Uncover local networking events, but only attend ones that are a tight fit in your niche. Otherwise, you can waste a ton of unproductive time on these.
- **Continually and relentlessly grow your generalist and moneyball skills; this cannot be overstated.**

While most of us don't want to limit our career choices by job title, industry, location, etc., it is vitally important to do so. This might seem counter to the advice I gave earlier that points to generalists being more valuable than specialists, but it is compatible nonetheless. If we don't limit our choices, at least for the current job search, we will spend way too much time going in a hundred different directions, and that does not serve us well, especially with how distracted we all are and how limited our time is to pursue a new job search. So don't be afraid of limiting yourself; narrow your focus of job search (titles, location, type of organization, industry, non-profit, for-profit, etc.) and stick to that for ninety days. It will take some discipline to not get distracted by some other shiny career idea, but if we challenge ourselves to stick with that focus for ninety days, it will either show some promise, perhaps by landing a few interviews (no guarantee of a job), or it will be nothing. If the former, consider further pursuing that angle or refining it slightly. If the latter, then rethink your focus completely and try for another ninety days.

> It's not who you know. It's who knows you.
>
> DANA VANDENHEUVEL

Networking, in a traditional sense, is changing. It used to be that you could network (or sleep) your way to the top, and to some extent, this is still true. But the fundamental change toward building authentic lifelong relationships will advance your career further than the old-school model of networking. Recognize the fact that early on your career you're more in a taking mode rather than a giving mode. Without experience in any field, you just don't have as much to offer. Because your network isn't as developed, you need recommendations to build credibility. You need to ask people in your network for connections for a job or a certain industry you're trying to get into or advice on how to write a resume or handle an interview. The challenge early in your career is to try to find ways to give other people something of value. It'll get progressively easier as you grow and mature in your career and your network connections grow. But you'll still have to be intentional about giving because things will get busier. Try to help connect others to good positions that advance their career; always ask yourself how you can serve others' interests, not just your own.

Most people you network with or who know you well won't be able to help you in your job search. Yep, you read that right; most of your network WON'T be able to help you find a job. Networking is important, but if you expect your friends and family to take the time to find you a job, you're probably going to be disappointed. Everybody is so busy with their own lives, even if they wanted to help, they often don't take the time. Or they don't seem to notice the connections they could make for you ... ones that would be perfect. That's not to say that all is lost and that we shouldn't use networking to find a job. It is just that we shouldn't have too high of an expectation that it will uncover a job for us. Instead, we should rely on them more for emotional support. Accept the fact that most people in your network that you reach out to in your job search will have NO idea how to help you connect with others in their network, even if they offer to. Either they won't understand your background and/or story, or they just aren't that well connected.

Don't be discouraged, but continue to work your network and look for that needle in the haystack. Ninety-nine percent of the people you connect with won't help you find a job, but it only takes one percent. It is our duty not to get discouraged, to continue networking, and persist to find a job. But regardless of whether or not others can help your search, you need to have a well-rehearsed elevator speech. This is simpler than you might think; it boils down to completing the following statements and then being able to rattle them of quickly and without hesitation. So give it a try, and practice it with some friends.

1. My name is ____.
2. My most recent position was ____ at ____.
3. My major responsibilities were ____.
4. Wherever I work, I bring three strengths: ____.

5. I am looking to _____ in the future.

A great way to make a habit of networking and collecting those contacts for use at a later date is LinkedIn. Develop a habit to make a 1st connection on LinkedIn with everyone you meet, whether you meet them initially in person, via phone, or e-mail. Looking them up right away on LinkedIn after your conversation and asking them to become a 1st connection will allow you to more quickly build your contact list. Make the connection request personal. Mention something about your interaction with them. Ultimately, longer term, you will be able to leverage your LinkedIn repository of connections to obtain other connections and specific knowledge. You will more easily stay in touch with people. LinkedIn can become a long-term strategy for managing your career, not a short-term strategy as most people are using it. Don't ask yourself how using LinkedIn can help you right now, but how it might help you in five, ten, or twenty years from now. Being willing to help your connections in their own job searches and candidate recruitment is a way to build goodwill and credibility with others.

So begin with the end in mind, as Stephen Covey taught us; build that network now, years before you need to access it, so that when you do need it, you will have a robust, rich connection list that you can leverage appropriately, not abusively. Then leverage it only when you need it most to find a job, recruit someone, or check uncommon references. There are all kinds of ways to use LinkedIn. If you are researching someone or some company and you notice that a trusted friend of yours has a connection, you can call that trusted friend and get the "skinny" on the person or organization. You can also use LinkedIn to uncover 1st or 2nd connections at an organization you desire to be employed at. This kind of information is invaluable and can only be obtained over time through a persistent, deliberate habit to acquire LinkedIn connections before you need them. So begin with the end in mind and develop that daily ritual to add anyone you meet, personally or professionally.

Organizations typically like to hire true insiders, people that rise up within the ranks, since they already know their leadership and working style and how they interact with people. They can observe this firsthand over time, making this a much lower risk than hiring an outsider. That's great if you're already an insider at the company you want to work at. But even if the job you're looking for is at another organization, you can position yourself as a pseudo-insider, lowering the perceived risk of the company you want to work at. If your connection (or hopefully, your connections, plural) can give you a strong, positive recommendation, it is much more likely that you can be hired. This is a tactic that has worked for me in my career, and something that will continue to be important as we all look for new ways to set ourselves apart in the job search. Many of us will have to face this prospect of getting hired as an outsider, since the pace and quantity of layoffs is increasing in the workforce. You have to leverage your contacts that either are working or used to work in the target organization, but make sure that you are not asking someone you barely know to put their reputation on the line for you. You have to develop the relationship, trust, and respect with that person long before you ever need to ask them for their help, so that when you do ask, they more than willing to oblige.

25

Resumes, Cover Letters, and Applicant Tracking Systems, Oh My!

An employer will not want to hire somebody who just wants a job. They will hire somebody who wants to work for them.

JAMES CAAN

When approaching an employer (whether via phone, e-mail, resume, social media, website) please ask yourself, "What's in it for them?" Anytime you're pitching somebody anything, whether it's in your career or asking somebody to do something, you must think this through first. Before you send that e-mail or make that phone call, ask yourself, "What's in it for them?" and pitch accordingly. And we shouldn't try to fool ourselves into thinking that we never sell or pitch anything; we do this each and every day in our personal lives (to our friends and family) and in our work lives (to our boss and peers) whether or not we are aware of it and whether or not we do a poor job at it. This is especially important when we are seeking a new position. We must resist the urge to sell them on how cool we think our skills and experience are. We need to pitch our candidacy based on what their perceive needs are. This comes from asking probing questions of the HR and/or hiring manager and reviewing the company website, press releases, and social media.

While there is no "right" way to compose a resume, I don't recommend using a simple chronological format. I prefer a functional resume, which allows you to focus on key functional areas of experience. You can then follow with a brief chronology as part of a functional resume. While you are working in a job, keep track of all of your accomplishments with specific data and metrics to add to your resume. Don't wait until you're looking for your next job to capture your accomplishments, since it will be hard to remember the specifics of what you accomplished. List very data-driven metrics of accomplishments like "Increased sales by X% over this X time period by my X action."

Be mindful of what you put on your resume. Think through how it might be perceived by others. I once put my personal e-mail address on my resume. Now, that is the right thing to do, but my personal e-mail address was gfunkdaddy@hotmail.com. (I no longer have this address, so please don't send me an e-mail there.) I didn't think about the fact that I was definitely giving the wrong impression to potential employers by putting that on my resume. Ironically, it did get me at least one interview that I likely wouldn't have gotten otherwise. I was interviewing for a job applying pest-control products at Terminix. After I landed the job, the managers admitted to me that they were intrigued by my resume, not because they thought I would be an exemplary employee, but because it was funny. So they said, "Hey, let's see what this guy looks like. This could be an interesting interview." I'm not sure what they thought they were going to experience when they interviewed me, but I was a lot different than what they had anticipated. I was courteous and professional, but I remember them telling me several months later that the interview was thought of initially as kind of a joke. And while this is a funny story that ultimately worked out for me, it could've ended up the opposite way, preventing me from even landing an interview. Hiring managers are always looking for some reason, however small, to rule out a candidate before the interview process even begins.

Take a customized approach for cover letters too, using language you find on the job posting, company website, and whatever you learn from talking to the recruiter (more on how to do this shortly). This includes learning more about the hiring manager from the recruiter, then scouring the internet for the hiring manager's hot buttons, and speaking to how you will help in those areas. I cannot emphasize strongly enough the importance of taking a highly customized approach.

Can't we do better with Applicant Tracking System (ATS) software? The task of wading through piles of resumes is different than it used to be. Many companies now use an ATS to screen and vet candidates. Most ATS software parses keywords from your cover letter, resume, and application to determine if you score high enough (somewhere in the top ten to twenty applicants is the cutoff line) for the hiring manager and recruiter to even review. This feature is understandably hated by most job seekers, since technology alone (not coupled with human interaction) tends to screen out people who could succeed at the job but don't fit the cookie cutter job description (years of experience, formal education, specific job titles, keyword density, etc.). But this is what most organizations use. We need to learn how to work within their system, so here are several key points to consider.

1. Consider using a service like Resunate to optimize your resume to the job description.
2. Always customize your resume for the organization and position. Take into consideration the culture and values of the organization as much as you do the position keywords.
3. Make sure to include keywords that you know are appropriate in your industry and are in the job description, but don't overdo it. The latter can get you kicked out as a keyword spammer. It needs to look natural to a human reader; otherwise, you are overdoing it.
4. Remove past positions that are irrelevant to this position.
5. Create a professional summary at the top to give the reader a high-level overview.
6. Bullet points are okay to use, but don't use other special characters.
7. Avoid fancy borders or shading.
8. Have an English pro proofread your resume for errors in spelling, punctuation, and grammar.
9. Remove unnecessary graphics or images, since this will confuse an ATS. (This can be hard for creative types, but this is the system we're dealing with.)
10. Upload a Word or text version of your resume, not a PDF, since the latter can't be parsed by most ATS.
11. Don't complete multiple applications for the same job; this will get the attention of the recruiter, but

not positive attention. It will annoy the heck out of them.

12. Applying to multiple positions within the same company is okay if you are truly qualified for multiple roles and you customize your resume for each. But be sure not to give conflicting information about things like salary requirements or years of experience, etc.

You may say, "Okay Miles, I have my resume and cover letter, but how do I avoid falling into the ATS black hole." While there is no magic formula that works every time, mainly because there are too many variables in play, here are a few steps you can take to increase your chances of getting an interview.

Find out who the recruiter is and reach out to them via e-mail asking for a brief phone call to understand a bit more about the job BEFORE you apply online. It may take some sleuthing to uncover the recruiter assigned to the position, but using LinkedIn, your network, and calling HR will usually help you identify this person. You are able to demonstrate your interest in the position by asking them questions about it. Try to understand the culture of the company and department, pay range, autonomy, unspoken responsibilities, and who the hiring manager is, etc. This allows you to show interest in THAT company and THAT job and puts you the top of the recruiter's mind. And you get to gain more info on the job, hiring manager, company, department, etc., which will better prepare you for the interview. Taking this action will increase your memorability and likelihood that they recommend your candidacy to the hiring manager beyond just a computer

(ATS) sorting through resumes to determine whether you have enough keywords in your resume and cover letter. Plus, it will highlight certain opportunities that you shouldn't even bother applying for. Whether or not you identify the recruiter, try to find someone at the organization that can hand deliver your resume (or forward it via e-mail). The fastest way to uncover someone you are connected with at another organization is to look up the company on LinkedIn and try to find a 1st or 2nd connection that you can reach out to. Ask if they will send your resume to the hiring manager, NOT the recruiter. The hiring manager is usually the final decision maker, not HR; the hiring manager, not the recruiter, has to work with the hire every day. Not only will passing your resume through someone in the company likely help you rise above the noise, but ATS software will usually score you higher as a result.

26

Loads of Questions to Ask

Now, you've got the interview for the job of your dreams, or at least so you think. You need to prepare for the interview. Research the company on their own website, LinkedIn, Glassdoor, Indeed, Google, etc. Missing this key preparation step will be obvious to your interviewer; trust me, I amazed at how many people forget this entirely or do a poor job. By researching the organization and industry, you prepare yourself to ask more intelligent questions, and the HR and hiring manager will take note. If you ask very few or no questions during your interview, you will appear as if you aren't interested in the position. While the HR person or team members you are interviewing with are important, if you can only impress one person, make it the hiring manager. Their opinion and vote will count more. And remember that the primary purpose of these questions is to help you understand whether the position will be a solid fit for you. The secondary purpose in asking intelligent questions to you show that you are the best fit from the employer's perspective. These are only suggestions, of course. You won't want to ask all of them every time; you will need to pick and choose depending on the circumstance. You may use some of them for separate rounds of interviews. Let's unpack some ideas on questions to ask, but keep in mind that these are only a starting point and are certainly not an exhaustive list.

1. What keeps you up at night? What is your worst business pain or fear?
2. Do you hire more for character or experience?
3. What percentage of your budget is used for professional development? [This is a relative measure and will indicate whether they value this sort of thing.]
4. Over what period of time will you monitor my initial performance? [This will uncover whether your boss has any unreasonable expectations of performance in a shorter period of time than you know it will take.]
5. How specifically will my performance be measured?
6. What is the number-one performance objective in the first ninety days? In the first twelve months?
7. What is your vision for the department and this role?
8. New or existing position?
    a) If new, what was the business pain that created this job?
    b) If existing, why is the previous person no longer here?
9. What are your pet peeves?
10. Who is your hero and why?
11. Am I taking over a struggling or succeeding department or company? [If you have the choice, you should take a challenging leadership role over an easy one. Following someone who didn't succeed is more preferable to a situation where you

have to follow someone successful. It is hard to fill the shoes of the latter.]

12. What percentage of the job is doing versus leading?
13. If I am selected as a final candidate, may I talk with a couple of key team members to get their view on the position and department?

Questions employers are asking themselves about you (you need to find a way to answer these whether or not they explicitly ask):

1. What financial success have they created?
2. How have their efforts been integral to that success?
3. Can they duplicate that here?
4. Will they fit with my team?

Questions to ask yourself before the interview:

1. Who is my Kryptonite? What type of boss makes me weaker or devalues my strengths? Knowing this will help you avoid a situation where you cannot be successful no matter how valuable your skills and experience are.
2. Should I accept this job? is a different question than "Why should I not accept this job?" They might seem like the same question, but they are different in the sense that the former will cause us to list the reasons to take the job, and the latter is more skeptical and causes more critical thinking about the things that aren't a good fit.

3. Why should I be nervous about the interview? Now, we will never rid ourselves of all nervousness, but it helps to consider that this might be the first interview for the hiring manager or recruiter, and they have human emotions too. They are relational, funny, compassionate, and engaging. And if they aren't, why would we want the job anyway?

Questions for our digital age

The following list of ten questions, created by Gordon Orr of McKinsey & Company, needs continual review throughout our career trajectory, whether just starting out or in the middle of a career. In my case, as a result of the shift to an even more digital age, I am adding significant specialist job skills in the area of digital marketing to my generalist leadership skill-set. Digital marketing is an area that will continue to grow and adapt, needing leaders who understand it and are constantly learning what is new in that field. But digital skills will need to be learned and added quickly to our tool belt, since every industry, not just marketing, is being impacted by this digital shift.

1. Am I obtaining the digital skills I need to land my first job and succeed at it?
2. What non-digital skills to I need to combine with my digital skills that will differentiate me?
3. How do I obtain these skills as early as possible?
4. Will the role that I am taking still exist in five years?
5. What roles will be in greater demand four years from now?

6. What digital skills will I need to succeed in these new roles?
7. How do I avoid becoming obsolete before I turn 35?
8. Is this a growth, mature, or declining industry, independent of digital's impact?
9. Where is this industry in its digital revolution?
10. Will this industry still exist ten years from now in a form that is recognizable to us today?

Questions for executives

Here are some questions to ask a board if you are being hired for an executive-level position that reports to the board. Make sure that you interview with the chairman or vice-chairman and at least one other board member to get a couple of different perspectives.

1. What does your board governance look like, and do you use Policy Governance®?
2. How much autonomy will I have?
3. How much debt and what type do you have? [This can highlight whether the organization is living beyond its means.]
4. What percentage of your budget is used for marketing (or insert your area of expertise here)? [This will show you how much they do or don't understand the amount of money needed to generate more money.]
5. May I interview a handful of staff to get their view of the organization?

Post Interview

Don't forget to send a written "Thank You" card to each interviewer (no e-mails unless it is in addition to a written one with additional info like a personal thank you video). This is especially important between multiple rounds of interviews; take the opportunity to show new information demonstrating you are a subject matter expert (article, video, portfolio, etc.) after each round of interviews. And follow up minimally by phone to show continued interest without coming off as desperate or a stalker.

27

Evaluating and Negotiating the Offer: Compensation, Benefits, and Intangibles

So much of our job search boils down to constraints: Where do we want to live? Where do we want our children to go to school? For-profit or not-for-profit organization? What industry do we want to be in? What functional discipline do we think best suits us? The challenge is that these are harder questions to answer than to ask. Make sure to consider these intangibles when considering a job offer. In the heat of the moment, we are flattered that we have been offered a position, especially in this economy, and we are tempted to take an offer that might not be the right fit even though the pay is good. Also, we might think we're worth a certain salary amount, but a lower salary might be okay in the presence of other intangibles like a good culture, work environment and decent benefits. These intangibles might outweigh less pay, longer commute, or something else we have to give up. There might be a situation that requires you to negotiate or even demand a higher salary and gold-plated benefits in certain industries. But by and large, we need to learn to be flexible and look at the entire compensation package (salary and benefits) and other intangibles (commute, environment, autonomy, working from home, etc.). Most of us would accept less salary and/or benefits in order to have other intangibles that make our lives and our family's lives less stressful and more enjoyable.

A bird in the hand is worth two in the bush.

In dealing with multiple interviews and/or offers, it can be tough to accept one offer while waiting on another offer or interview. But you should strongly consider accepting an offer even if there is another interview upcoming, since you don't want to risk alienating the current offering organization. When you get a job offer, don't be afraid to negotiate a bit. The company has indicated they want to hire you. That said, depending on how much work experience and/or leverage you have, don't play hardball either. If you are truly desperate for a job, do your best not to let your potential employer perceive that; otherwise, you will have less negotiating power. I'm not saying that you should never turn down an offer in hand because you have an upcoming interview that you are more excited about, but it is dangerous to either turn it down or delay giving the first offering organization your decision too much. And if you hold out too long, they may get cold feet and rescind their offer. Here are fifteen rules for negotiating a job offer, according to Deepak Malhotra:

1. Don't underestimate the importance of likability.
2. Help them understand why you deserve what you're requesting.

3. Make it clear they can get you.
4. Understand the person across the table.
5. Understand their constraints.
6. Be prepared for tough questions.
7. Focus on the questioner's intent, not on the question.
8. Consider the whole deal.
9. Negotiate multiple issues simultaneously, not serially.
10. Don't negotiate just to negotiate.
11. Think through the timing of offers.
12. Avoid, ignore, or downplay ultimatums of any kind.
13. Remember, they're not out to get you.
14. Stay at the table.
15. Maintain a sense of perspective.[7]

The height of your salary and how hard you negotiate on your total compensation package will dictate to some extent how your performance is perceived. Being underpaid isn't all that bad. In some cases, it may be preferable to being overpaid. Just think about it for a minute. If you have a higher salary relative to others in an organization, your boss is going to expect more of you. If you're a tough negotiator and you negotiate for a high salary or even a bonus, and maybe some extra weeks of vacation, you're always going to have a hard time performing at such a high level so as to justify your compensation. Alternatively, if you don't negotiate as hard but fight for what's fair and nothing out of the ordinary, you're not going to have as high of a bar to achieve. You'll have more opportunity to continue to grow in your salary. So it's a delicate balancing act: You don't want to give up on negotiating—I always try to get the best deal—but it's something that you have to be very mindful of in terms of how hard you negotiate. Generally speaking, pay at non-profits is less than at similarly sized for-profit organizations, so by default, people that work at non-profits are underpaid. Most people who go to work for non-profits are either sold out to the mission or want an easier job, but not necessarily less talented then those who work at for-profits. For all the talk about pay and benefits being highly important, there are many other intangible things to consider in a workplace environment. Most people just want to be on a winning team or department, surrounded by people who have what it takes to win and succeed.

28

I Got The Job;
How Do I Keep It?

Anyone who has traveled internationally more than once or twice will tell you that it is wise to learn the ways or culture of the country you're traveling to. The same applies to organizational culture. To be successful, one must understand the political and positional seats of power and the cultural norms. Some political/positional seats of power within an organization may lie within a departmental function. It might be marketing if the director of marketing has control over a large budget, which often determines the sales or the revenue the organization. In a non-profit, the seat of power could be the development department, since they bring in the money. Or a strong positional seat of power could be in Human Resources, since they control who gets hired and fired and what policies and procedures dictate how the organization is going to work and its culture. There is usually a financial seat of power that can dictate how money is spent within the organization. Other times it is a finance or accounting professional, like a controller or accounting manager that has a cost-cutting mindset instead of a growth mindset. They are not always going to look at things in terms of an investment in growth but how to minimize costs across the board. You can also have a top IT professional that won't allow certain projects to move forward, which can cause problems if other departments need it in order to work efficiently.

Be careful about giving too much of your opinion in the first ninety to one hundred twenty days of a job. We need to learn the ways the company does things, the how and why they do what they do, before we give an opinion about what we think should be changed. If there are obvious things that need to change, it is fine to recommend those, but be cautious, as some of our instincts may be inaccurate once we learn more about the idiosyncrasies and differences of our new organization. We tend to assume that our new organization is exactly like the last. Our enthusiasm often leads to resistance from company insiders who resent a know-it-all who disrespectfully challenges their view of the world. That assumption and approach can lead to misunderstanding at best and termination of employment at worst. So be sensitive to an organization's culture, especially when you are new on the job. That doesn't mean you have to agree with everything that the organizational culture deems appropriate. But you do you have to line up with it, or the culture will soon spit you out (translation: you will lose your job). Respect and blend in with the culture when you are new; then once you become more established and respected by the culture, you can attempt to change things. Trying to do the opposite will likely get you reprimanded or fired.

The top executive in an organization, whether that is Executive Director, CEO, President, General Manager, etc., will value the functional area they came from and undervalue areas they know nothing or little about. You should look at what positions they have been in before and what functional areas they come from (marketing, sales, development, finance, IT, human resources, etc.). That's important to understanding how they're going to react in their role as well as what they're going to value. Naturally, if they have experience in one of those areas more than another, they're going to give that more value. Any of these scenarios has implications for how money gets spent, what projects get green-lit, and what is valued in an organization. Becoming aware of these functional and positional seats of power will help us enormously to successfully navigate our career.

When presented with an open door, drive a Mack truck through it.

Also, be cautious how and when you spend your political capital. You have some credibility based on your past experience (unless this is your first job) and the fact that they selected you above all other candidates. So if you have had a couple of jobs, you bring credibility and expertise to the organization, but you need to be careful to use that wisely. This doesn't mean being too afraid and timid; you do need to take some risks. There is a window of time in the beginning where you can use some of that political capital or goodwill to try some things and challenge some boundaries. Be bold, but don't reach too far and lose the trust and credibility you are building with your supervisor. There is a delicate balance between asking for forgiveness versus knowing where you need to ask permission. This is something that is learned, and the more expertise you bring to the table, the more ability you're going to have to make decisions and changes more quickly. Questions to ask yourself about spending political capital are:

1. Have I earned enough credibility to use it?
2. Is this the right timing?
3. How should I use it?
4. How much or little should I use?

All of those questions are important to assess in any organization. We don't want to spend too much political capital too quickly. But we also should recognize that there is a time, especially at the beginning of a job, when we have to strike while the iron is hot, making changes to use that capital before we lose the "I'm new here" excuse. This allows us to take advantage of an opportunity to advance more of our agenda before more rigid norms develop. The US Presidency is a great example of this. A president who just won an election is in a position to push his agenda, which is why the first one hundred days of a presidency are usually a whirlwind of policy innovation. Some presidents spend their post-election capital more wisely than others. They understand when to use their political capital and do so in a requisite amount based on the situation. This is a very visible example that we all can recall, but this happens on a daily basis within many organizations. Those in positions of leadership may have to wait to advance their agenda because they have little political capital. Or they might have the capital, but it is unwise to expend it at this time. Waiting for a more opportune time in the future makes more strategic sense. At the same time, beginning in a new job requires us to build political capital as quickly as possible with our boss, peers, and subordinates. In other words, you need to find quick ways to build up some significant political capital through positive, meaty (not hollow) accomplishments. Manage that political capital, both at the beginning of a new job, throughout the lifecycle of your current job, and ultimately, throughout your career.

29

Closing Thoughts:
Don't Forget to Relax and
Have Fun

You might be thinking to yourself, "Holy crap, man; there are a million things I need to change and start or stop doing. There aren't enough hours in the day." The truth is that you are absolutely right. Trying to do too many things all at once will only stress you out even more and drive you to be less effective, even though you may becoming a workaholic at job seeking. So how do we balance things? Consider these recommendations:

- Limit the amount of hours spent seeking a job, depending on whether you currently have a job or other responsibilities. If you are unemployed, consider 25-30 hours a week; 40 might be too much. If you have a job, keep your search to a minimum, since the more you search for a new job, the harder it will be to keep that a secret from your current employer and the harder it will be for your mind not to wander during your workday.
- Structure some downtime for physical, mental, and emotional rest (besides sleep, which you need, too). Some possibilities are reading, meditation,

journaling, prayer, volunteering, hobbying, fixing up things around the house, spending time with spouse or family. Just make sure that, as much as finding a job shouldn't consume too much time, neither should rest time.

Frodo: I wish the ring had never come to me. I wish none of this had happened.

Gandalf: So do all who live to see such times. But that is not for them to decide. All we have to decide is what to do with the time that is given to us. There are other forces at work in this world, Frodo, besides the will of evil. Bilbo was meant to find the Ring. In which case, you were also meant to have it. And that is an encouraging thought.

FROM *THE LORD OF THE RINGS: THE FELLOWSHIP OF THE RING* (2001)

We may wish to return to simpler times, but as with all history, we tend to romanticize the past at the expense of the present. We have a choice to pine for the good ol' days or embrace Becoming Generation Flux. The challenging career landscape job seekers face is more complex than even a few years ago, but we have decisions and actions still within our control. There is hope! We should seize the day in areas we control and cede stress in areas we have no power. The bottom line is that it takes a lot of hard work and some luck to find a job that is truly meaningful and rewarding and pays you well. Many of us may have to work more than one job, perhaps a 9-to-5 job and a freelance job or multiple part-time jobs, or some combination thereof. Some may have to work a less-than-desirable shift: second, third, or swing shift instead of first shift. We may have to look for a new job every few years. We may have to take a step back or sideways in our career to learn and move forward. But in all of these scenarios, we must never forget that it is better than being unemployed.

> **President Snow:** Hope. It is the only thing stronger than fear. A little hope is effective. A lot of hope is dangerous.
>
> FROM *THE HUNGER GAMES*

Most companies or departments that are struggling and in need of a turnaround cannot see it. They are definitely not self-aware and just don't get it. I've been hired by four different companies that all needed someone to come in and turn things around, only one of which really understood that fact. So in our job search, we shouldn't allow ourselves to get discouraged when people don't find what we have to offer valuable, even though it may be precisely what they need. Many people are just blind to what they need. I would encourage us to continue to focus on what we're truly energized and passionate about and don't let go of those. We should seek positions and organizations that need those skills that energize us, whether the organization realizes it or not, rather than try to conform to a role that doesn't challenge us just for the safety and comfort of a paycheck. Even though it is more challenging to find that kind of a job, it is infinitely more rewarding.

> No matter what they say, you always have a choice. You just don't always have the guts to make it.
>
> RAY N. KUILI, *AWAKENING*

Far too often we naively and unintentionally hand over the pen of our lives and allow other people to write the chapters of our life's story. Why should we let our boss, friends, family, or coworkers write our story? Others only have the power to write your story if you let them have that power. We may think, "Well, my boss (or my parents or my spouse or somebody) has authority and control over me," and to some extent that is true. But they only have as much power and control as we give them. So write your own story, chart your own course, and don't use others' positional power as an excuse for not living life to the fullest. Will you seize the pen and write your own story?

My Current and Forthcoming Books and Resources

Why Leadership Sucks Volume One: Fundamentals of Level 5 Leadership and Servant Leadership

Currently available online in ebook, paperback, and audio book formats

> "It is literally true that you can succeed best and quickest by *helping* others to succeed."

(AUTHOR NAPOLEON HILL)

What is leadership? How do we define leadership? What is servant leadership? What are the most effective leadership characteristics? Do you wish your company had a leadership development program, or are you frustrated with organizational leadership? Do you wonder why some leadership styles suck? You are not alone.

So why does leadership suck? It sucks because real leadership is hard, requires selfless service, and because the buck stops with you. Servant leadership or Level 5 leadership is uncomfortable, humbling, self-denying, painful, and counterintuitive. Nonetheless, it is the only kind of leadership that brings lasting results, genuine happiness, and true self-fulfillment.

If you haven't read volume one of the *Why Leadership Sucks* series, be sure to pick it up!

Why Leadership Sucks Online Video Course

Currently available at Udemy.com

Miles and Christopher Paul Elliott will guide your leadership journey to increase leadership IQ and enhance effectiveness using real-world examples. Chris is a servant leadership speaker and author of *Thought Shredder*. Video sessions include: Self-Awareness, First Impressions Are Lasting Impressions... As Long As You Let Them Last, and Are you a Micromanager or a Macromanager?

If you enjoyed either volume one or two of the Why Leadership Sucks books, plug into these thirty-three lectures with a full ninety minutes of video packed with actionable insights, bonus MP3s, PowerPoints, and other resources.

The Serial Specialist: Who They Are and Why You MUST Hire Them to Thrive

"The division of labour offers us the first example of how, as long as man remains in natural society, that is as long as a cleavage exists between the particular and the common interest, as long therefore as activity is not voluntarily, but naturally, divided, man's own deed becomes an alien power opposed to him, which enslaves him instead of being controlled by him. For as soon as labour is distributed, each man has a particular, exclusive sphere of activity, which is forced upon him and from which he cannot escape."

(SOCIALIST KARL MARX)

"Specialization may be all well very well if you happen to have skills particularly suited to these jobs, or if you are passionate about a niche area of work, and of course there is also the benefit of feeling pride in being considered an expert. But there is equally the danger of becoming dissatisfied by the repetition inherent in many specialist professions…

"Moreover, our culture of specialization conflicts with something most of us intuitively recognize, but which career advisers are only beginning to understand: we each have multiple selves… We have complex, multi-faceted experiences, interests, values and

165

talents, which might mean that we could also find fulfillment as a web designer, or a community police officer, or running an organic cafe.

"This is a potentially liberating idea with radical implications. It raises the possibility that we might discover career fulfillment by escaping the confines of specialization and cultivating ourselves as wide achievers ... allowing the various petals of our identity to fully unfold."

(PHILOSOPHER ROMAN KRZNARIC)

Do you hire specialists in your specific industry but continually feel disappointed with their innovation and creativity levels? Are you routinely rejecting generalists for fear of them not sticking around very long? Or are you frustrated with your own career, sensing a kind of indentured servitude to your particular work specialty? Do you yearn to do other things? Do you get bored after a few years in one type of work?

If so, *The Serial Specialist* is for you. Miles will help you understand why these outliers are typically outcasts but should be brought into your corporate fold to achieve success in this challenging economy. You will learn why you and they are to be highly valued, and how to identify, hire, and retain adaptable, agile, and innovative talent.

Coming soon

The Opportunity Cost of Christ

"We drive our cars 60-70 miles per hour with an oncoming car doing the same with only a white line and six to eight feet separating us. We place our faith that every car will not cross into our lane. We fly on airplanes that take us over oceans, trusting the pilots with our very lives. We ride on thrilling amusement rides that take us several stories into the air and travel fifty to seventy miles per hour down a winding slope. We trust the operators of that ride with our own mortality.

"There is a great irony in the fact that we can place our faith in such things but cannot place our faith in the hands of our Creator."

(OS HILLMAN, TAKEN FROM MARKETPLACELEADERS.ORG)

We all have faith and trust in many features of modern life, seeking the allusion of security. Among them are a paper money system, accumulated wealth, relationships, food, alcohol, government, business, and education. We even believe that the brakes on our cars will stop us and that doctors will heal our ailments. So why do we have such a hard time putting our faith and trust in Christ?

My forthcoming book, *The Opportunity Cost of Christ*, argues that trusting in and following Christ is not a leap of faith in defiance of reason, but the reasonable conclusion of a rational mind.

Coming soon

Career Books I Recommend

- *ThoughtShredder* by Christopher Paul Elliott
- *Ubiquity: Why Catastrophes Happen* by Mark Buchanan
- *Antifragile: Things That Gain From Disorder* by Nassim Nicholas Taleb
- *Quitter: Closing the Gap Between Your Day Job and Your Dream Job* by Jon Acuff
- *The Two-Income Trap: Why Middle-Class Parents Are Going Broke* by Elizabeth Warren and Amelia Warren Tyagi
- *Moneyball: The Art of Winning an Unfair Game* by Michael Lewis
- *Don't Go Back to School* by Kio Stark
- *The Higher Education Bubble* by Glenn Harlan Reynolds
- *The Essential Guide for Hiring and Getting Hired* by Lou Adler
- *Purple Squirrel: Stand Out, Land Interviews, and Master the Modern Job Market* by Michael B. Junge
- *The 4-Hour Workweek* by Timothy Ferriss
- *One Big Thing: Discovering What You Were Born to Do* by Phil Cooke
- *48 Days to the Work You Love* by Dan Miller
- *Start: Punch Fear in the Face, Escape Average, and Do Work That Matters* by Jon Acuff

- *The First 90 Days* by Michael D. Watkins
- *The Start-up of You: Adapt to the Future, Invest in Yourself, and Transform Your Career* by Reid Hoffman
- *Lynchpin* by Seth Godin
- *Now, Discover Your Strengths* by Marcus Buckingham
- *How Successful People Think* by John C. Maxwell
- *Getting Things Done: The Art of Stress-Free Productivity* by David Allen
- *What Color is Your Parachute?* by Richard N. Bolles
- *How to Fail at Almost Everything* by Scott Adams

About the Author

Miles Anthony Smith, an ambivert and serial specialist, has held senior, executive leadership positions for businesses and non-profits over the past fifteen years. He has broad management skills across many functional business disciplines in accounting, finance, human resources, marketing, and leadership, earning a Bachelor of Music Composition degree from Oral Roberts University and a master's in Business Administration from Oklahoma State University. Miles currently works for Imaginasi-com as director of digital marketing. Miles is the author of the *Why Leadership Sucks* and the *Why Career Advice Sucks* series.

Born a Hoosier, raised an Okie, and currently residing in the frozen tundra of Green Bay, Wisconsin, Miles is happily married to Carolyn and is a proud father of three. Now in his mid-thirties, he was fortunate to have been given a significant leadership opportunity by his father at the age of twenty-five. He is a classically trained violist, violinist, and composer, with passions in the fields of small-business management, marketing, macroeconomics, servant leadership, and classical education.

Miles, a Generation X leader and author, cares enough about organizational health to make the tough decisions, hire and coach the right people, set clear expectations, develop a strong team culture, and strengthen organizational cash flow, exhibiting both humility and fierce resolve. His mission in life is: "To chart the course, pave the pathway, and light the lane for others to eclipse my own success in leadership."

Notes

1   Dwyer, Debra and Jianting Hu (2000). "Retirement Expectations and Realizations: the Role of Health Shocks and Economic Factors," in *Forecasting Retirement Needs and Retirement Wealth*, Mitchell, Olivia, P. Brett Hammond and Anna Rappaport, eds.

2   Jones, Landon (1980), *Great Expectations: America and the Baby Boom Generation*, New York: Coward, McCann and Geoghegan.

3   http://www.economist.com/blogs/prospero/2010/10/waiting_superman

4   http://www.usatoday.com/story/money/personalfinance/2013/09/18/how-much-of-a-pay-raise-can-you-expect-in-2014/2832791/

5   http://marlagottschalk.wordpress.com/2014/02/12/the-poor-fit-6-signs-that-your-job-is-absolutely-the-wrong-one/

6   Coile, Courtney B. and Phillip B. Levine (2009). "The Market Crash and Mass Layoffs: How the Current Economic Crisis May Affect Retirement," presented at NBER Summer Institute Workshop on Aging, July 21–25, 2009.

7   http://hbr.org/2014/04/15-rules-for-negotiating-a-job-offer/ar/1

www.ingramcontent.com/pod-product-compliance
Lightning Source LLC
Chambersburg PA
CBHW031934190326
41519CB00007B/527